Rand McNally

HISTORICAL ATLAS OF THE WORLD

CONTENTS

Copyright © 1991
Rand McNally
Educational Publishing Division
P.O. Box 1906
Skokie, Illinois 60067-8906

Reorder #528-17756-7
Edited by DR. R.R. Palmer
Revision and Production/Instructional Design Associates (IDeA)
and Katherine Townes Books, Boulder, Colorado
5th printing - 1995

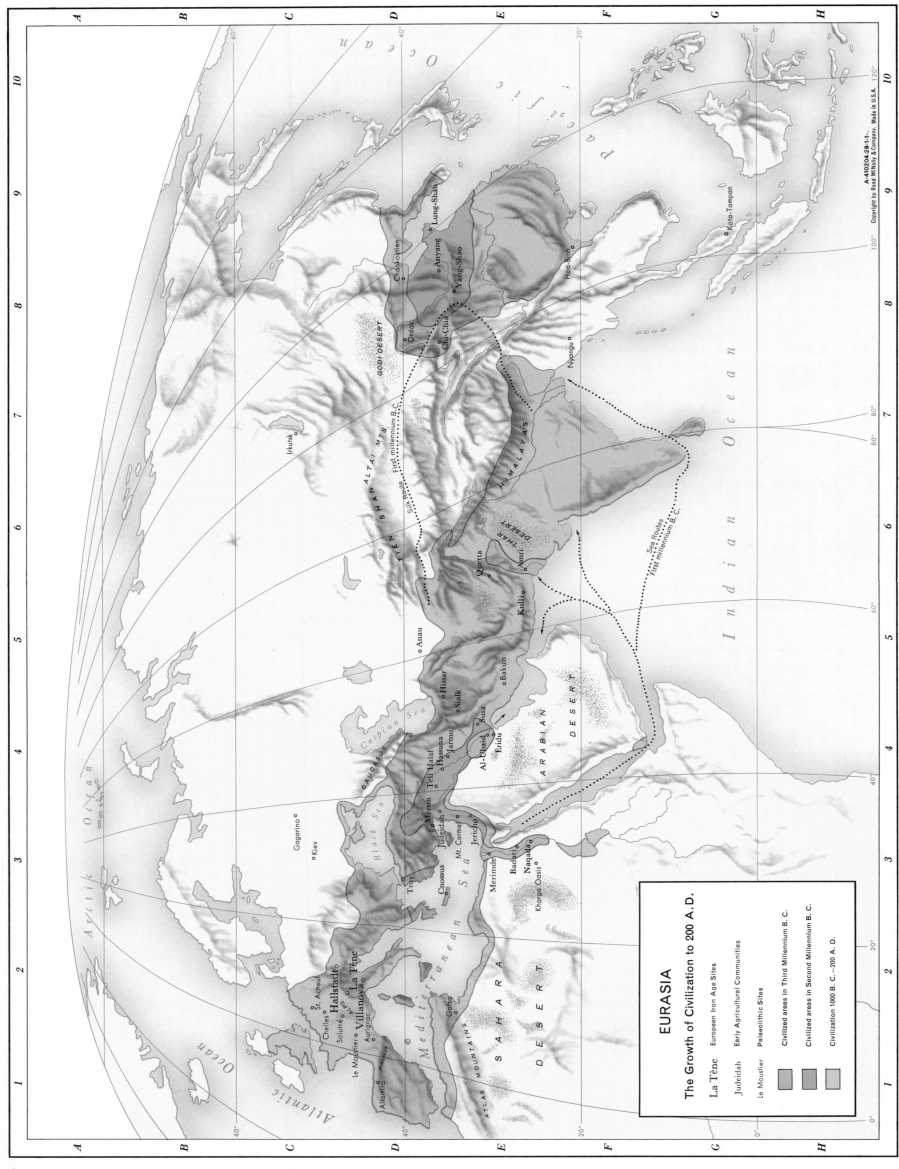

EURASIA

The Growth of Civilization to 200 A.D.

La Tène	European Iron Age Sites
Judeidah	Early Agricultural Communities
le Moustier	Palaeolithic Sites

Civilized areas in Third Millennium B. C.

Civilized areas in Second Millennium B. C.

Civilization 1000 B. C.–200 A. D.

A-410204-2B-1-1-. Copyright by Rand McNally & Company. Made in U.S.A.

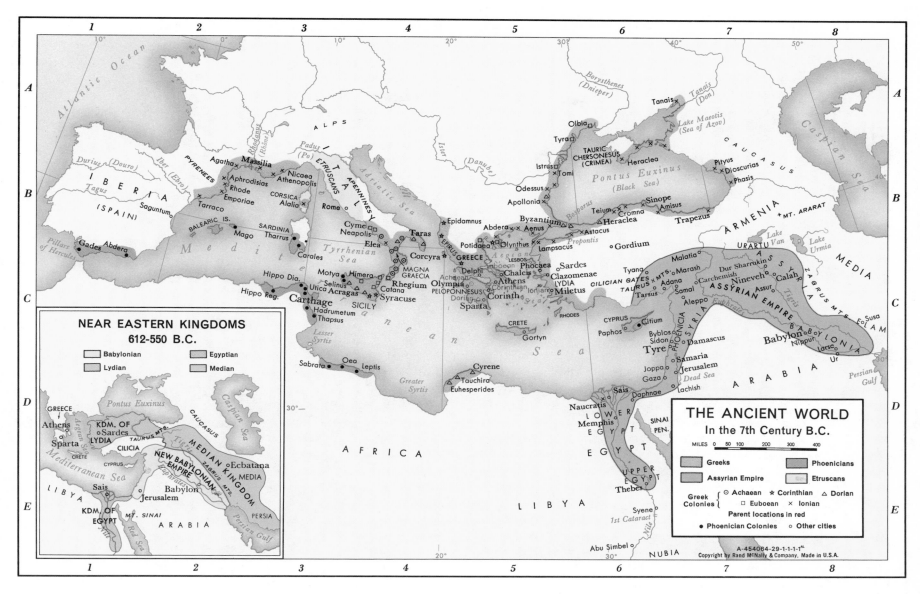

THE ANCIENT WORLD
In the 7th Century B.C.

MILES 0 50 100 200 300 400

Greeks	Phoenicians
Assyrian Empire	Etruscans

Greek Colonies: ◎ Achaean ★ Corinthian △ Dorian □ Euboean × Ionian

Parent locations in red

● Phoenician Colonies ○ Other cities

A-454064-29-1-1-1-1⁴⁰
Copyright by Rand McNally & Company, Made in U.S.A.

NEAR EASTERN KINGDOMS 612-550 B.C.

Babylonian	Egyptian
Lydian	Median

Labels on main map include:
Atlantic Ocean, ALPS, IBERIA (SPAIN), Durius (Douro), Tagus, Iber (Ebro), PYRENEES, Saguntum, Tarraco, Emporiae, Rhode, Aphrodisias, Agatha, Massilia, Nicaea, Athenopolis, BALEARIC IS., Mago, SARDINIA, Thurros, CORSICA, Alalia, Rome, ETRUSCANS, APENNINES, Adriatic Sea, Padus (Po), Cyme, Neapolis, Elea, Taras, Tyrrhenian Sea, Carales, Motya, Selinus, Acragas, Catana, Himera, Rhegium, MAGNA GRAECIA, SICILY, Syracuse, Hippo Dia., Utica, Hippo Reg., Carthage, Hadrumetum, Thapsus, Lesser Syrtis, Greater Syrtis, Sabrata, Oea, Leptis, Gades, Abdera, Pillars of Hercules, Mediterranean Sea, AFRICA, LIBYA, Cyrene, Tauchira, Euhesperides, Naucratis, Sais, LOWER EGYPT, Memphis, SINAI PEN., UPPER EGYPT, Thebes, Syene, 1st Cataract, Abu Simbel, NUBIA, Corcyra, EPIRUS, GREECE, Delphi, Olympia, PELOPONNESUS, ACHAEAN, DORIAN, Corinth, Sparta, CRETE, Gortyn, RHODES, CYPRUS, Paphos, Citium, Byblos, Sidon, PHOENICIA, Tyre, Damascus, Samaria, Jerusalem, Dead Sea, Joppa, Gaza, Lachish, Daphnae, ARABIA, Aegean Sea, Chalcis, Phocaea, Sardes, Clazomenae, LYDIA, Miletus, Athens, IONIA, Corinthian, Epidamnus, Abdera, Aenus, Potidaea, Olynthus, Lampsacus, Propontis, Byzantium, Bosporus, Astacus, Teium, Heraclea, Cromna, Sinope, Amisus, Trapezus, ARMENIA, MT. ARARAT, URARTU, Lake Van, Lake Urmia, MEDIA, Caspian Sea, Pontus Euxinus (Black Sea), Apollonia, Odessus, Tomi, Istrus, Tyras, Olbia, Borysthenes (Dnieper), Tanais, Lake Maeotis (Sea of Azov), TAURIC CHERSONESUS (CRIMEA), Heraclea, Pityus, Dioscurias, Phasis, CAUCASUS, Tanais (Don), Ister (Danube), Gordium, Tyana, TAURUS MTS., CILICIAN GATES, Adana, Tarsus, Samal, Marash, Malatia, Carchemish, Aleppo, ZAGROS MTS., Nineveh, Assur, Calah, Dur Sharrukin, ASSYRIAN EMPIRE, SYRIA, Euphrates, Tigris, Babylon, Nippur, Larsa, Ur, BABYLONIA, ELAM, Susa, Persian Gulf

Near Eastern Kingdoms inset labels:
GREECE, Athens, Sparta, Crete, CYPRUS, Mediterranean Sea, LIBYA, Sais, Jerusalem, KDM. OF EGYPT, MT. SINAI, ARABIA, Red Sea, Pontus Euxinus, KDM. OF LYDIA, Sardes, CILICIA, TAURUS MTS., CAUCASUS, Caspian Sea, MEDIAN KINGDOM, Ecbatana, MEDIA, NEW BABYLONIAN EMPIRE, Babylon, Tigris, Euphrates, ZAGROS MTS., PERSIA, Persian Gulf

---

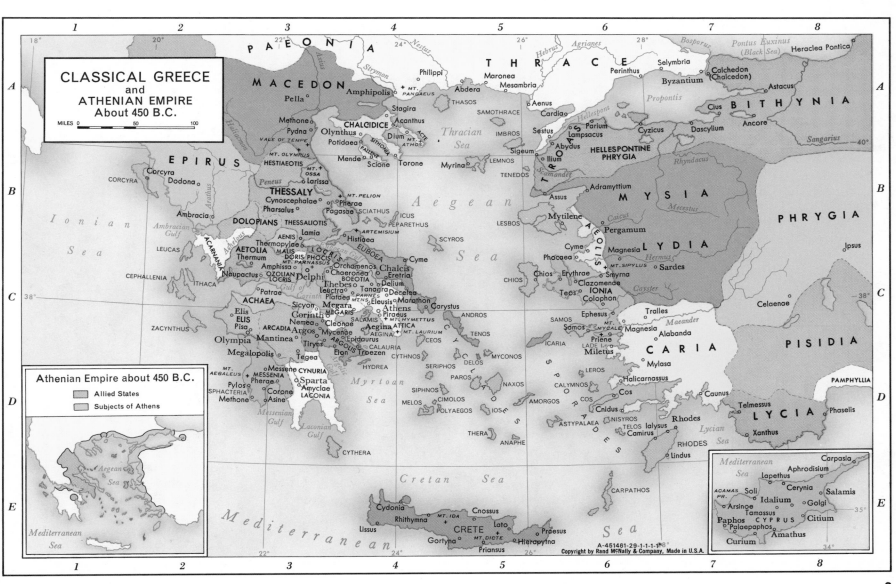

CLASSICAL GREECE and ATHENIAN EMPIRE About 450 B.C.

MILES 0 50 100

Athenian Empire about 450 B.C.

Allied States	Subjects of Athens

A-451461-29-1-1-1-1⁴⁸
Copyright by Rand McNally & Company, Made in U.S.A.

Labels on Classical Greece map include:
PAEONIA, MACEDON, Pella, Amphipolis, Philippi, MT. PANGAEUS, THRACE, Maronea, Mesambria, Abdera, Aenus, Cardia, Perinthus, Selymbria, Byzantium, Calchedon (Chalcedon), Astacus, BITHYNIA, Ancore, Cius, Dascylium, Propontis, Bosporus, Pontus Euxinus (Black Sea), Heraclea Pontica, Sangarius, EPIRUS, CORCYRA, Corcyra, Dodona, Ambracia, Ambracian Gulf, LEUCAS, CEPHALLENIA, ITHACA, ZACYNTHUS, Ionian Sea, THESSALY, HESTIAEOTIS, MT. OLYMPUS, VALE OF TEMPE, MT. OSSA, Larissa, Cynoscephalae, Pharsalus, Pherae, MT. PELION, Pagasae, SCIATHUS, PERRHAEBIA, DOLOPIANS, THESSALIOTIS, Methone, AENIS, MALIS, Lamia, Thermopylae, Amphissa, AETOLIA, Thermum, DORIS, PHOCIS, LOCRIS, OZOLIAN LOCRIS, Naupactus, Delphi, MT. PARNASSUS, ACHAEA, Patrae, Aegium, Cynoscephalae, Stagira, CHALCIDICE, Acanthus, Olynthus, Potidaea, SITHONIA, PALLENE, Mende, Scione, Torone, ACTE, MT. ATHOS, THASOS, Thracian Sea, SAMOTHRACE, IMBROS, LEMNOS, Myrina, TENEDOS, Sigeum, Ilium, Abydos, Lampsacus, Parium, Cyzicus, HELLESPONT, HELLESPONTINE PHRYGIA, Adramyttium, Assus, MYSIA, Pergamum, AEOLIS, Mytilene, LESBOS, Magnesia, MT. SIPYLUS, Sardes, LYDIA, PHRYGIA, Ipsus, Rhyndacus, Caicus, Hermus, Cayster, Maeander, Cyme, Phocaea, Smyrna, Erythrae, Clazomenae, Teos, Colophon, IONIA, Ephesus, CHIOS, Chios, ICARIA, SAMOS, Samos, MT. MYCALE, Priene, Miletus, Magnesia, Tralles, Alabanda, Celaenae, CARIA, Mylasa, Halicarnassus, Caunus, PISIDIA, PAMPHYLIA, LYCIA, Telmessus, Xanthus, Phaselis, Lycian Sea, RHODES, Rhodes, Lindus, Camirus, Ialysus, TELOS, NISYROS, ASTYPALAEA, Cos, COS, CALYMNOS, LEROS, AMORGOS, IOS, POLYAEGOS, CIMOLOS, MELOS, THERA, ANAPHE, CARPATHOS, EUBOEA, Histiaea, ARTEMISIUM, Chalcis, Eretria, BOEOTIA, Orchomenos, Thebes, Tanagra, Delium, Leuctra, Plataea, Chaeronea, Coronea, MT. PARNES, MT. CITHAERON, Decelea, Marathon, Eleusis, MEGARIS, Megara, Athens, Piraeus, ATTICA, MT. HYMETTUS, MT. LAURIUM, Aegina, AEGINA, CALAURIA, Troezen, Epidaurus, ARGOLIS, Mycenae, Tiryns, Argos, Nemea, Cleonae, Corinth, Sicyon, Gulf of Corinth, ARCADIA, Mantinea, Tegea, Megalopolis, ELIS, Elis, Pisa, Olympia, CYNURIA, MESSENIA, Messene, Pherae, Pylos, SPHACTERIA, Corone, Asine, Methone, MT. AEGALEUS, LACONIA, Sparta, Amyclae, Gytheum, Messenian Gulf, Laconian Gulf, CYTHERA, Myrtoan Sea, Aegean Sea, ANDROS, TENOS, CEOS, CYTHNOS, SERIPHOS, SIPHNOS, PAROS, NAXOS, DELOS, MYCONOS, SPORADES, SCYROS, ICUS, PEPARETHUS, Cretan Sea, CRETE, Cydonia, Lissus, Rhithymna, MT. IDA, Cnossus, Lato, Praesus, Gortyna, Hierapytna, MT. DICTE, Priansus, Mediterranean Sea

Cyprus inset labels:
Mediterranean Sea, ACAMAS PR., Soli, Lapethus, Cerynia, Aphrodisium, Carpasia, Arsinoe, Idalium, Golgi, Salamis, Paphos, Palaepaphos, CYPRUS, Citium, Amathus, Tamassus, Curium

Athenian Empire inset labels:
Aegean Sea, Mediterranean Sea

3

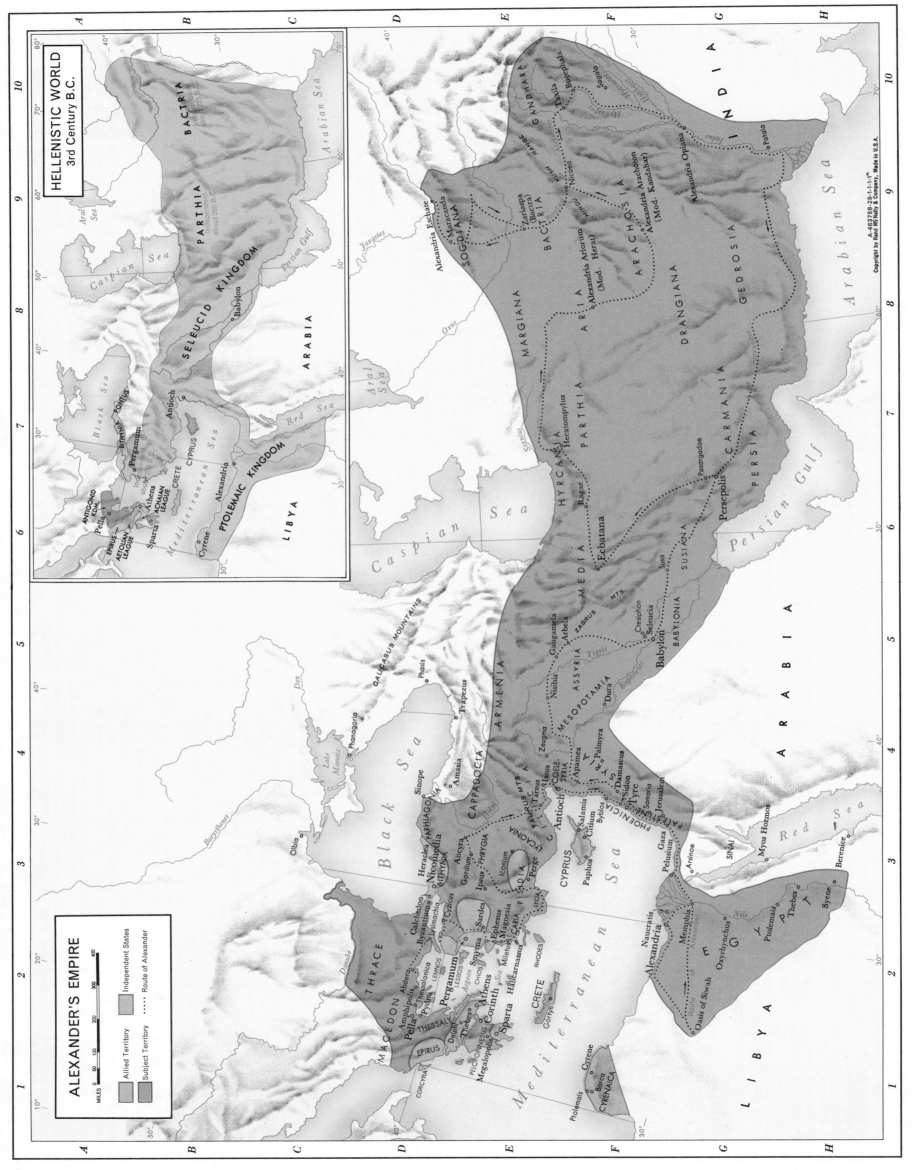

HELLENISTIC WORLD
3rd Century B.C.

Aral Sea

BACTRIA *independent about 250 B.C.*

PARTHIA *independent about 250 B.C.*

Arabian Sea

Caspian Sea

SELEUCID KINGDOM

Babylon

Antioch

PONTUS

BITHYNIA

Pergamum

CYPRUS

CRETE

Athens

Sparta

ACHAEAN LEAGUE

ANTIGONID KGM.

Pella

EPIRUS

AETOLIAN LEAGUE

Cyrene

Alexandria

PTOLEMAIC KINGDOM

Mediterranean Sea

Black Sea

Red Sea

Persian Gulf

ARABIA

LIBYA

ALEXANDER'S EMPIRE

Allied Territory

Subject Territory

Independent States

······ Route of Alexander

MILES
0 50 100 200 300 400

INDIA

GANDHARA

Taxila

Bucephala

Sagala

Indus

Hydaspes

HINDU KUSH RANGE

SOGDIANA

Alexandria Eschate

Maracanda

Zariaspa (Bactra)

BACTRIA

Nicaea

ARIA

Alexandria Ariorum

Alexandria (Mod. Herat)

ARACHOSIA

Alexandria Arachoton (Mod. Kandahar)

Alexandria Opiana

DRANGIANA

GEDROSIA

Patala

Arabian Sea

MARGIANA

Oxus

Jaxartes

HYRCANIA

Hecatompylus

PARTHIA

Ragae

Rhagae

Ecbatana

MEDIA

CARMANIA

PERSIA

Pasargadae

Persepolis

Susa

SUSIANA

BABYLONIA

Ctesiphon

Seleucia

Babylon

Tigris

Euphrates

ZAGRUS MTS.

ASSYRIA

Nisibis

Gaugamela

Arbela

MESOPOTAMIA

Dura

ARMENIA

Zeugma

Apamea

Palmyra

COELE SYRIA

Damascus

Sidon

Tyre

PHOENICIA

PALESTINE

Jerusalem

Gaza

Pelusium

Arsinoe

Caspian Sea

CAUCASUS MOUNTAINS

Phasis

Trapezus

Phanagoria

Don

Lake Maeotis

Olbia

Borysthenes

Black Sea

Sinope

Amasia

PAPHLAGONIA

CAPPADOCIA

Halys

Heraclea

Nicomedia

BITHYNIA

Ancyra

Gordium

PHRYGIA

Iconium

TAURUS MTS.

CILICIA

LYCAONIA

PISIDIA

Tarsus

Issus

Antioch

Salamis

Citium

CYPRUS

Paphos

Byblos

Damascus

SYRIA

Myos Hormos

Berenice

Syene

Thebes

EGYPT

Ptolemais

Oxyrhynchus

Nile

Memphis

Alexandria

Naucratis

Oasis of Siwah

Route of Alexander

SINAI

Red Sea

ARABIA

Calchedon

Byzantium

THRACE

Abdera

Amphipolis

Thessalonica

Pydna

MACEDON

Pella

THESSALY

Delphi

Thebes

EPIRUS

Corinth

Athens

Megara

PELOPONNESUS

Megalopolis

Sparta

Corcyra

CORCYRA

LEMNOS

LESBOS

CHIOS

Smyrna

Ephesus

Sardes

Magnesia

Miletus

CARIA

Halicarnassus

LYDIA

Perge

LYCIA

RHODES

CRETE

Gortyn

Aegean Sea

Cyrene

Barca

CYRENAICA

Ptolemais

Pergamum

Pitane

Cyzicus

Lampsacus

LIBYA

Mediterranean Sea

A-463758-29-1-1-1-1™
Copyright by Rand McNally & Company, Made in U.S.A.

INDIA 250 B.C. AND 400 A.D.

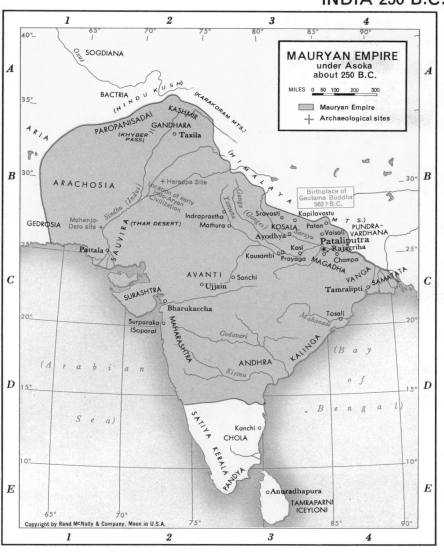

MAURYAN EMPIRE
under Asoka
about 250 B.C.

MILES 0 50 100 200 300

- Mauryan Empire
- ✛ Archaeological sites

SOGDANA
Oxus
BACTRIA
(HINDU KUSH)
(KARAKORAM MTS.)
ARIA
KASHMIR
PAROPANISADAI
(KHYBER PASS)
GANDHARA
• Taxila
ARACHOSIA
(HIMALAYA)
+ Harappa Site
Location of early
Indo-Aryan
civilization.
Birthplace of
Gautama Buddha
563? B.C.
GEDROSIA
Mohenjo-
Daro site +
(THAR DESERT)
Indraprastha
Mathura
Srāvasti
Kapilavastu
Patan
KOSALA
Ayodhya
Vaisali
PUNDRA-
VARDHANA
Pattala
Kasi
Kausambi
Prayaga
Rajagriha
Pataliputra
MAGADHA
Champa
VANGA
SURASHTRA
AVANTI
Sanchi
Ujjain
SAMATATA
Bharukaccha
Tamralipti
MAHARASHTRA
Godavari
Mahanadi
Tosali
Surparaka
(Sopara)
ANDHRA
KALINGA
(Bay
Kistna
of
(Arabian
Bengal)
Sea)
SATIYA
KERALA
Kanchi
CHOLA
PANDYA
Anuradhapura
TAMRAPARNI
(CEYLON)

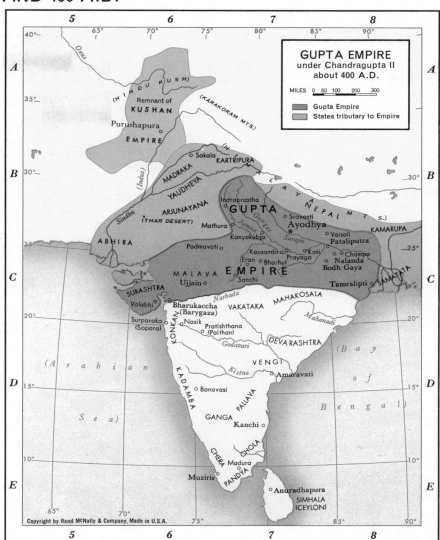

GUPTA EMPIRE
under Chandragupta II
about 400 A.D.

MILES 0 50 100 200 300

- Gupta Empire
- States tributary to Empire

Oxus
(HINDU KUSH)
Remnant of
KUSHAN
Purushapura
EMPIRE
(KARAKORAM MTS.)
(Indus)
Sakala
KARTRIPURA
MADRAKA
YAUDHEYA
NEPAL
Indraprastha
ARJUNAYANA
GUPTA
Sravasti
KAMARUPA
Sindhu
(THAR DESERT)
Mathura
Kanyakubja
Ayodhya
Vaisali
ABHIRA
Padmavati
Kausambi
Prayaga
Kasi
Pataliputra
Champa
Eran
Bharhut
Nalanda
MALAVA
EMPIRE
Bodh Gaya
SURASHTRA
Ujjain
Sanchi
Tamralipti
SAMATATA
Valabhi
Bharukaccha
(Barygaza)
Narbada
VAKATAKA
MAHAKOSALA
Nasik
Surparaka
(Sopara)
Pratishthana
(Paithan)
Mahanadi
KONKAN
DEVA RASHTRA
Godavari
VENGI
KADAMBA
Kistna
Amaravati
(Arabian
Banavasi
(Bay
Sea)
GANGA
PALLAVA
of
Kanchi
Bengal)
CHERA
Madura
Muziris
CHOLA
PANDYA
Anuradhapura
SIMHALA
(CEYLON)

Copyright by Rand McNally & Company. Made in U.S.A.

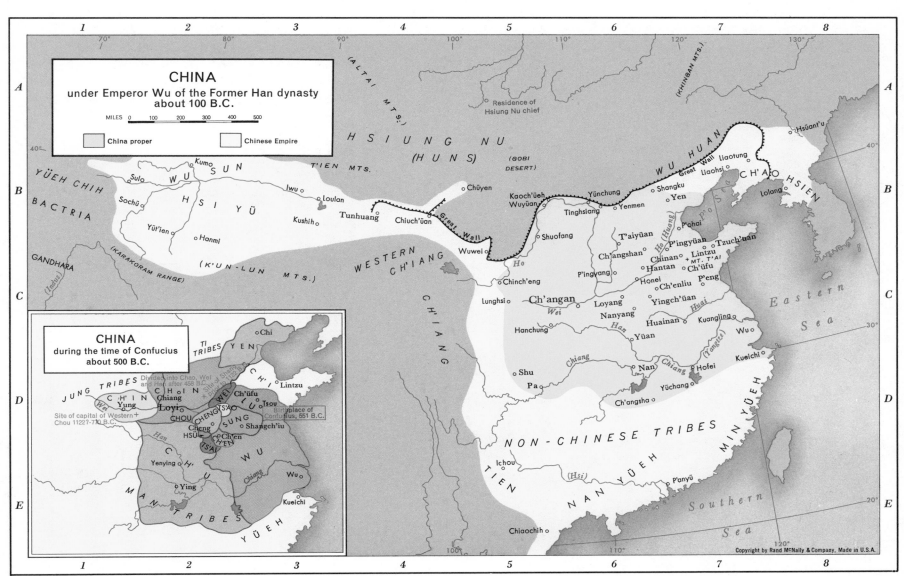

CHINA
under Emperor Wu of the Former Han dynasty
about 100 B.C.

MILES 0 100 200 300 400 500

- China proper
- Chinese Empire

(ALTAI MTS.)
(KHINGAN MTS.)
Residence of
Hsiung Nu chief
HSIUNG NU
(HUNS)
(GOBI DESERT)
WU HUAN
Hsüant'u
YÜEH CHIH
(TIEN MTS.)
Kumo
WU SUN
Sula
Iwu
Chüyen
Kaoch'üeh
Yünchung
Great Wall
Liaotung
Liaohsi
CH'AO HSIEN
BACTRIA
Sochü
HSI YÜ
Loulan
Wuyüan
Yenmen
Shangku
Yen
Lolang
Yüt'ien
Kushih
Tinghsiang
Shangku
Po Sea
GANDHARA
(Indus)
Hanmi
Tunhuang
Chiuch'üan
Great Wall
Shuofang
T'aiyüan
Ch'angshan
Chihan
P'ingyüan
Lintzu
MT. T'AI
Tzuch'uan
(KARAKORAM RANGE)
(K'UN-LUN MTS.)
Wuwei
Ho (Hwang)
Hantan
Ch'üfu
WESTERN CHIANG
Chinch'eng
Ho
P'ingyang
Honei
Ch'enliu
P'eng
Eastern
Lunghsi
Ch'angan
Loyang
Yingch'üan
Sea
CHIANG
Wei
Nanyang
Huainan
Kuangling
Wu
Hanchung
Han
Yüan
Huai (Yangtze)
Kueichi
Shu
Nan
Chiang
Hofei
Pa
Yüchang
NON-CHINESE TRIBES
Ch'angsha
Chiang
MIN YÜEH
TIEN
Ichou
NAN YÜEH
Southern
Chiaochih
(Hsi)
P'anyü
Sea

CHINA
during the time of Confucius
about 500 B.C.

TI TRIBES
YEN
Chi
JUNG TRIBES
CH'IN
CH'I
Lintzu
Divided into Chao, Wei
and Han after 458 B.C.
Site of Shang
capital c. 1300 B.C.
Wa
Yung
CHIN
Chiang
Site of capital of Western
Chou 1122?-770 B.C.
CHENG
TSAO
Tsou
Ch'üfu
LU
Birthplace of
Confucius, 551 B.C.
Loyi
CHOU
Cheng
HSÜ
CH'EN
Shangch'iu
TS'AI
WEI
CH'U
SUNG
WU
Yenying
Ying
MAN TRIBES
Chiang
Wu
Kueichi
YÜEH

Copyright by Rand McNally & Company. Made in U.S.A.

5

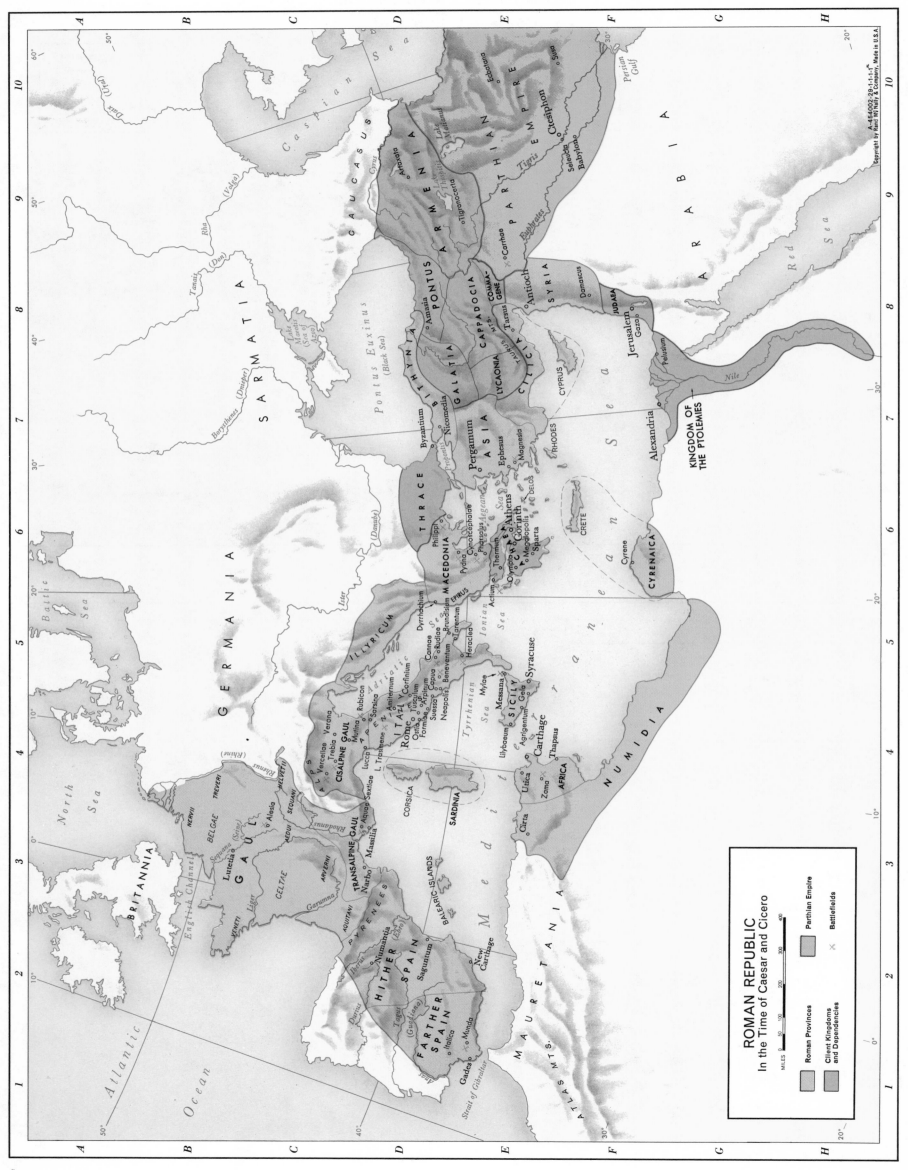

ROMAN REPUBLIC
In the Time of Caesar and Cicero

MILES 0 50 100 200 300 400

| | Roman Provinces | | Parthian Empire |
| | Client Kingdoms and Dependencies | × | Battlefields |

A-454002-29-1-1-1-1ᴬ
Rand McNally & Company, Made in U.S.A.
Copyright by

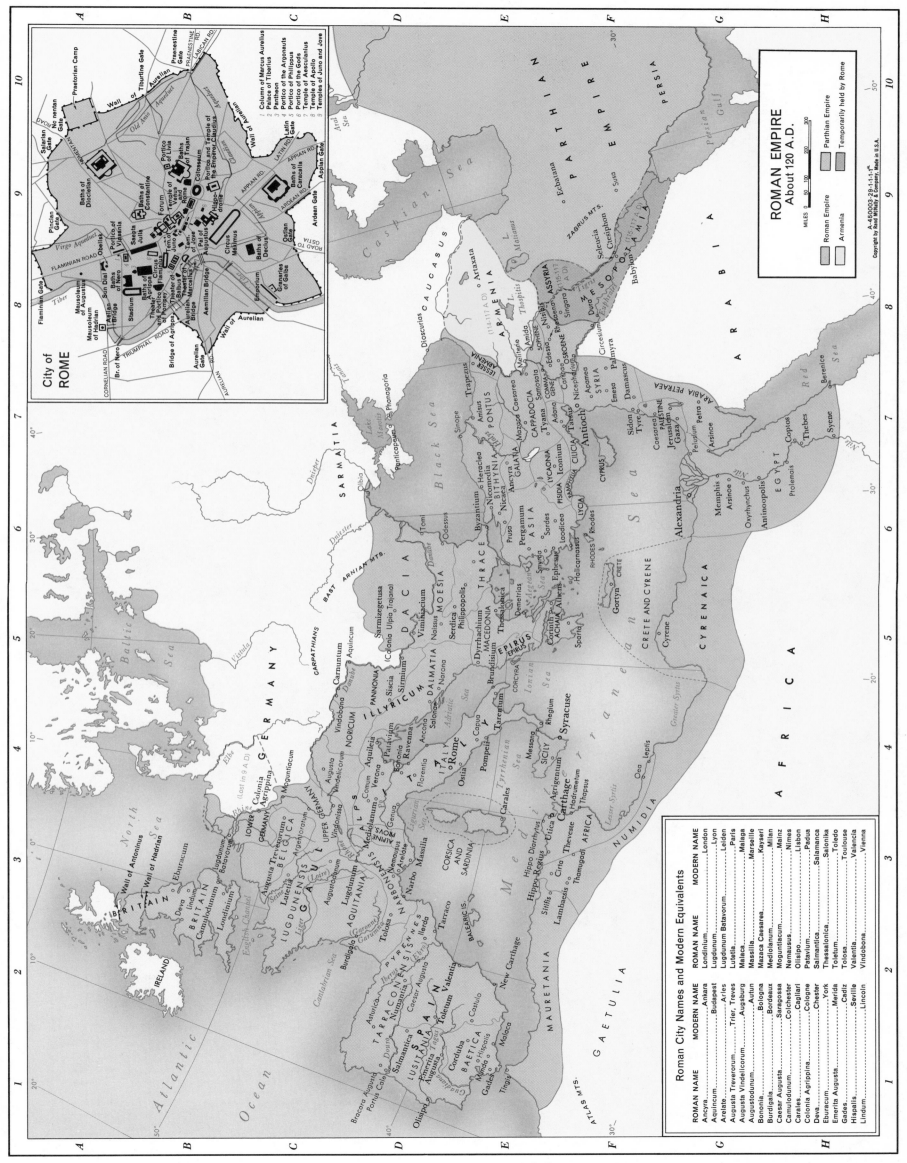

City of ROME

1 Column of Marcus Aurellus
2 Palace of Tiberius
3 Pantheon
4 Portico of the Argonauts
5 Portico of Philippus
6 Portico of the Gods
7 Temple of Aesculanius
8 Temple of Apollo
9 Temples of Juno and Jove

ROMAN EMPIRE
About 120 A.D.

MILES 0   50 100   200   300

Roman Empire

Armenia

Parthian Empire

Temporarily held by Rome

A-450003-29-1-1-1-A
Copyright by Rand McNally & Company, Made in U.S.A.

Roman City Names and Modern Equivalents

ROMAN NAME	MODERN NAME	ROMAN NAME	MODERN NAME
Ancyra	Ankara	Londinium	London
Aquincum	Budapest	Lugdunum	Lyon
Arelate	Arles	Lugdunum Batavorum	Leiden
Augusta Treverorum	Trier, Treves	Lutetia	Paris
Augusta Vindelicorum	Augsburg	Malaca	Malaga
Augustodunum	Autun	Massilia	Marseille
Bordigala	Bordeaux	Mazaca Caesarea	Kayseri
Burdigala	Bordeaux	Mediolanum	Milan
Caesar Augusta	Saragossa	Moguntiacum	Mainz
Camulodunum	Colchester	Nemausus	Nimes
Carales	Cagliari	Olisipo	Lisbon
Colonia Agrippina	Cologne	Patavium	Padua
Deva	Chester	Salamantica	Salamanca
Eburacum	York	Thessalonica	Salonika
Emerita Augusta	Merida	Toletum	Toledo
Gades	Cadiz	Tolosa	Toulouse
Hispalis	Seville	Valentia	Valencia
Lindum	Lincoln	Vindobona	Vienna

7

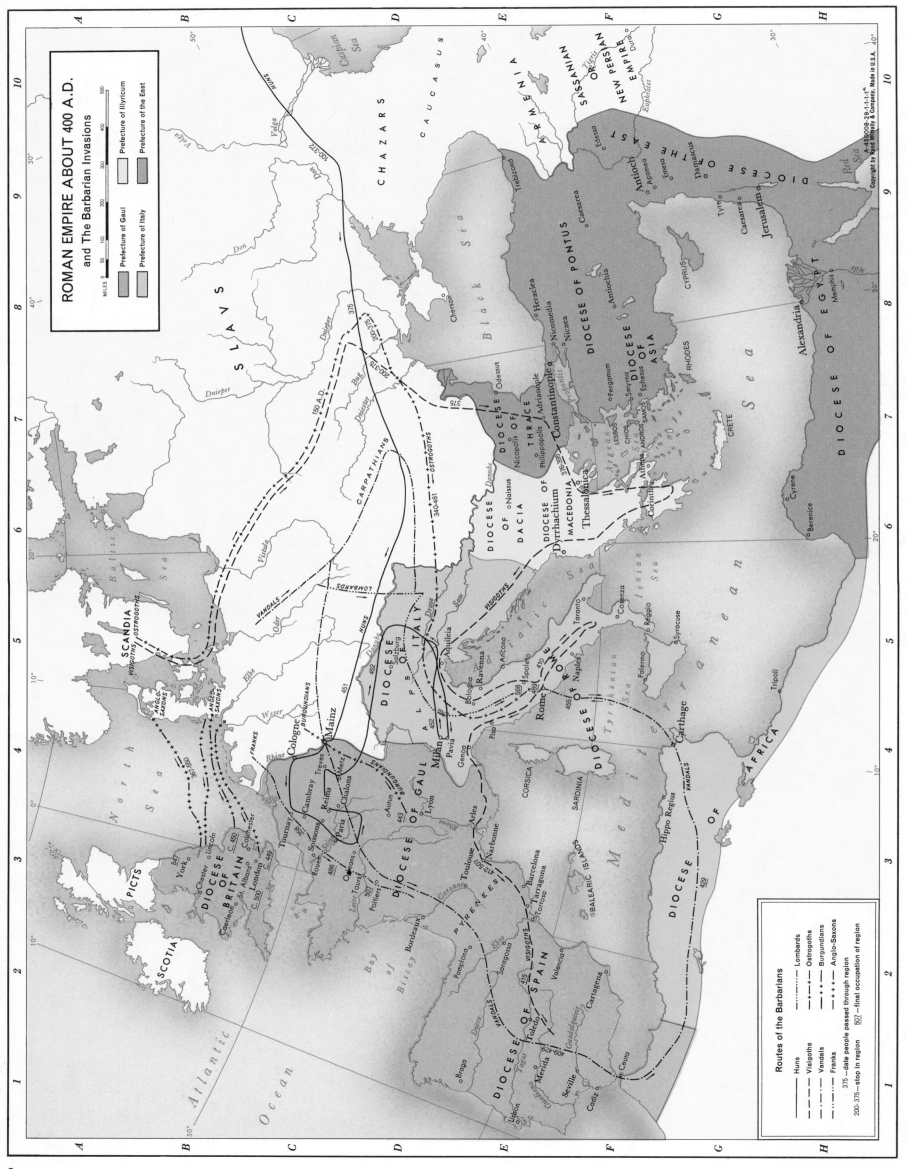

ROMAN EMPIRE ABOUT 400 A.D.
and The Barbarian Invasions

MILES
0 50 100 200 300 400 500

| Prefecture of Gaul | Prefecture of Illyricum |
| Prefecture of Italy | Prefecture of the East |

Routes of the Barbarians

Huns	Lombards
Visigoths	Ostrogoths
Vandals	Burgundians
Franks	Anglo-Saxons

375—date people passed through region
200-375—stop in region   507—final occupation of region

A-48Q00B-29-1-1-1-'44
Copyright by Rand McNally & Company. Made in U.S.A.

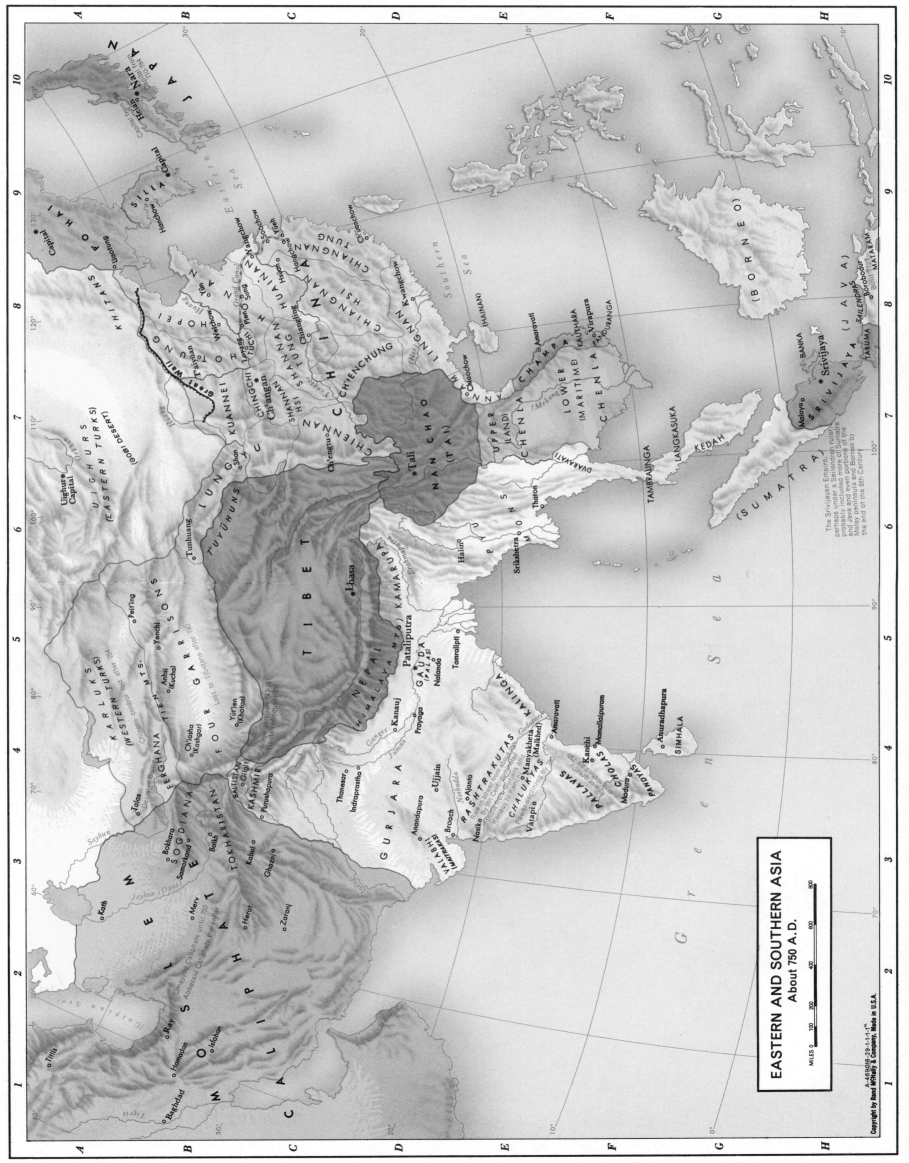

EASTERN AND SOUTHERN ASIA
About 750 A.D.

MILES 0 100 200 400 600 800

The Srivijayan Empire,
perhaps under a Sailendran ruler,
probably included more of Sumatra
and Java and even portions of the
Malay peninsula and Borneo by
the end of the 8th Century

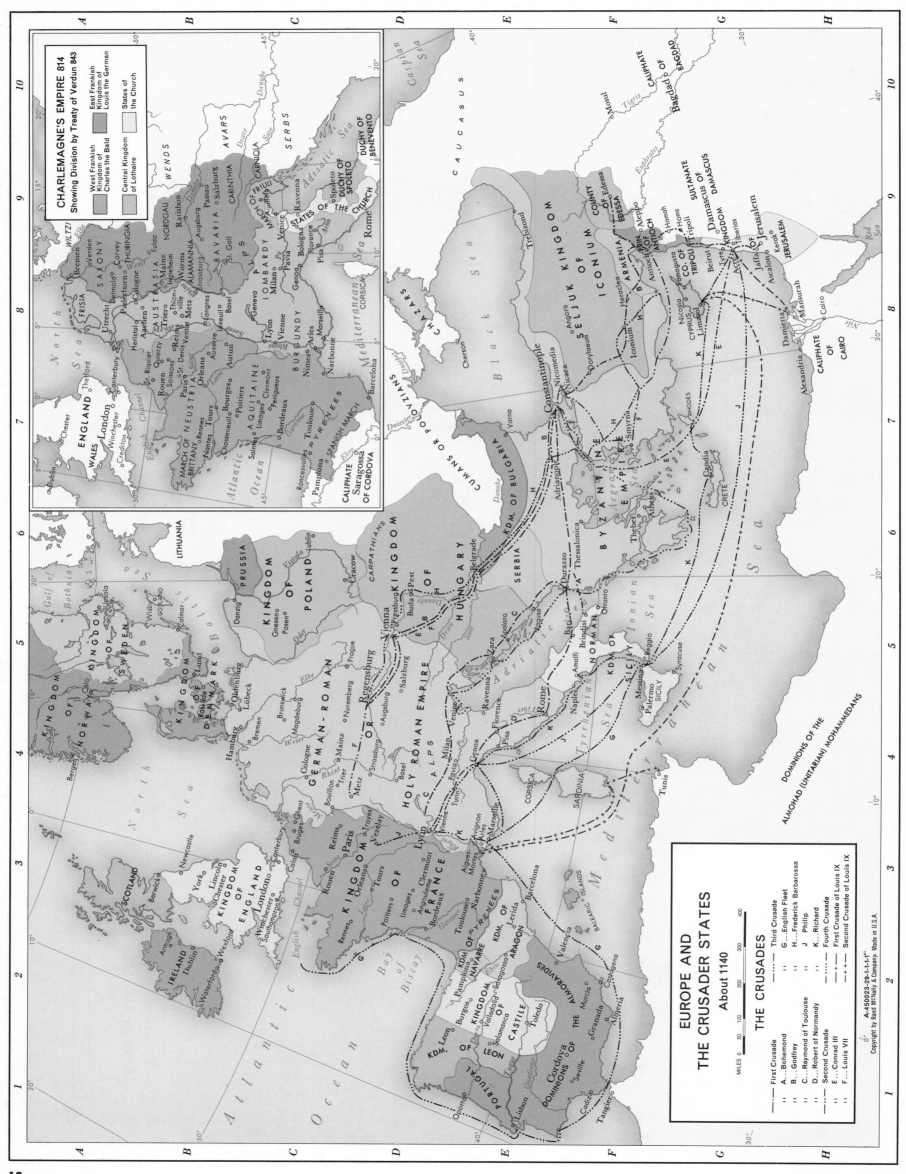

CHARLEMAGNE'S EMPIRE 814
Showing Division by Treaty of Verdun 843

West Frankish
Kingdom of
Charles the Bald

East Frankish
Kingdom of
Louis the German

Central Kingdom
of Lothaire

States of
the Church

EUROPE AND
THE CRUSADER STATES
About 1140

THE CRUSADES

— · — · —	First Crusade	— · · · —	Third Crusade
— · · —	A...Bohemond	" "	G...English Fleet
" "	B...Godfrey	" "	H...Frederick Barbarossa
" "	C...Raymond of Toulouse	" "	J...Philip
" "	D...Robert of Normandy	" "	K...Richard
— · · · · —	Second Crusade	— + — + —	Fourth Crusade
" "	E...Conrad III	— + + — + +	First Crusade of Louis IX
" "	F...Louis VII	" "	Second Crusade of Louis IX

MILES 0 50 100 200 300 400

A-450023-20-1-1-1-1³¹
Copyright by Rand McNally & Company. Made in U.S.A.

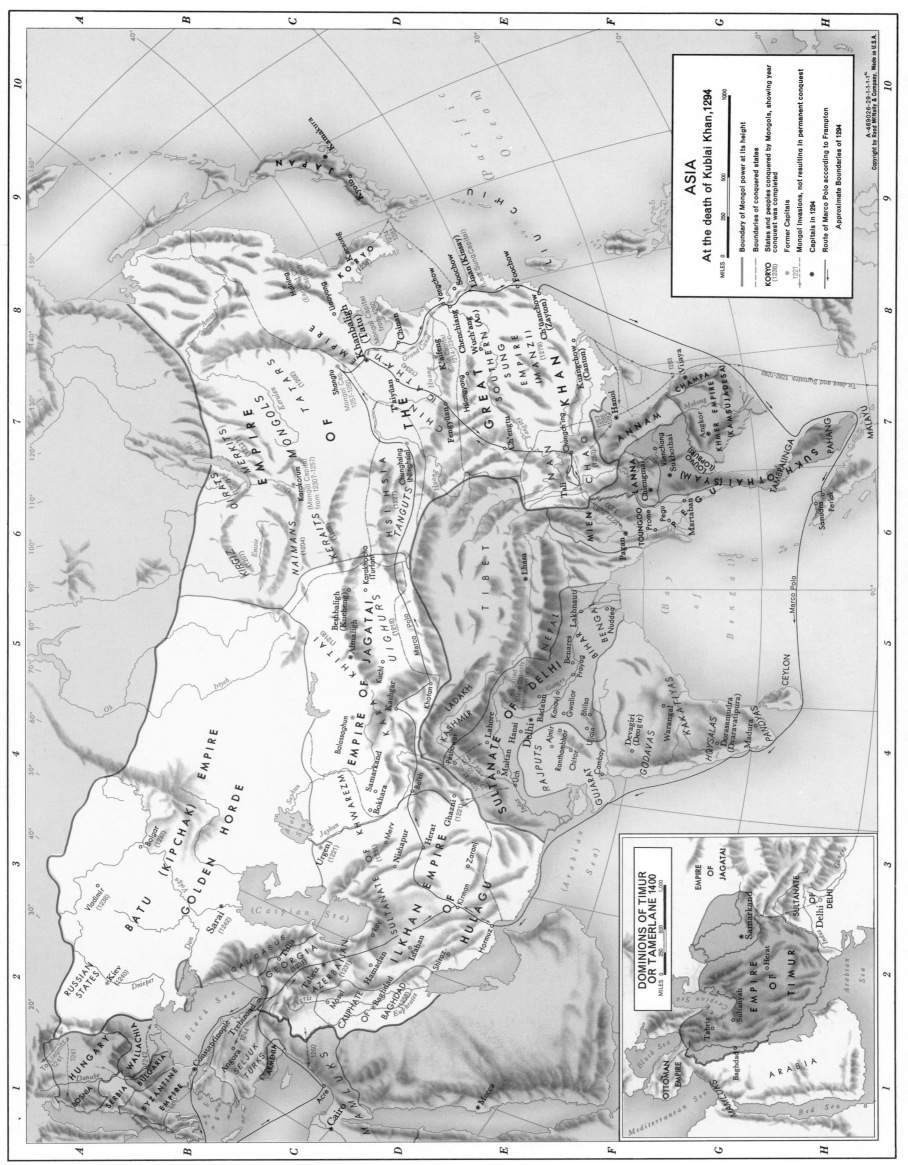

ASIA
At the death of Kublai Khan, 1294

MILES 0   250   500   1000

——— Boundary of Mongol power at its height

——— Boundaries of conquered states

——— Boundaries of conquered states conquest was completed

States and peoples conquered by Mongols, showing year conquest was completed

KORYO (1236)   Former Capitals

 ⊛   Mongol Capitals

1221   Mongol invasions, not resulting in permanent conquest

 ✳   Capitals in 1294

→   Route of Marco Polo according to Frampton

——— Approximate Boundaries of 1294

A-469026-29-1-1-1-1"
Copyright by Rand McNally & Company. Made in U.S.A.

DOMINIONS OF TIMUR OR TAMERLANE 1400

MILES 0   250   500   1000

EMPIRE OF JAGATAI

SULTANATE OF DELHI

EMPIRE OF TIMUR

Samarkand
Tabriz
Sultaniyeh
Herat
*Delhi
Baghdad

OTTOMAN EMPIRE
MAMLUKS
ARABIA

Black Sea
Caspian Sea
Arabian Sea
Mediterranean Sea
Red Sea

11

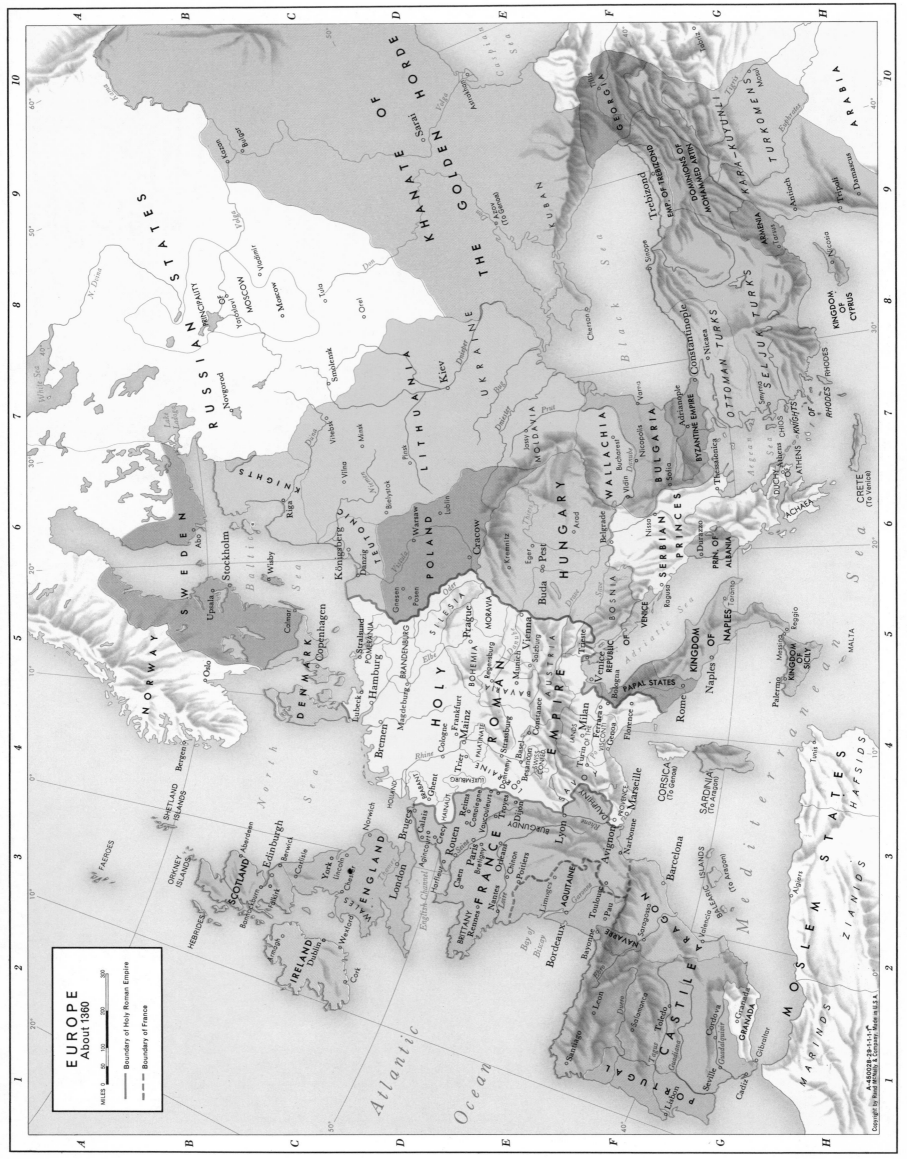

EUROPE
About 1360

MILES 0 50 100 200 300

—— Boundary of Holy Roman Empire
- - - Boundary of France

A 450028-29-1-1-1-1*
Copyright by Rand McNally & Company. Made in U.S.A.

RUSSIAN STATES

KHANATE OF THE GOLDEN HORDE

NORWAY

SWEDEN

DENMARK

SCOTLAND

ENGLAND

IRELAND

WALES

FRANCE

HOLY ROMAN EMPIRE

POLAND

LITHUANIA

UKRAINE

TEUTONIC KNIGHTS

HUNGARY

BOHEMIA

MORAVIA

SILESIA

POMERANIA

BRANDENBURG

BAVARIA

AUSTRIA

SWISS CONFED.

LORRAINE

PALATINATE

SAVOY

DAUPHINY

PROVENCE

BURGUNDY

AQUITAINE

NAVARRE

CASTILE

PORTUGAL

ARAGON

GRANADA

MOSLEM STATES

MARINIDS ZIANIDS HAFSIDS

PAPAL STATES

KINGDOM OF NAPLES

KINGDOM OF SICILY

VENICE

REPUBLIC OF VENICE

BOSNIA

SERBIAN PRINCES

WALLACHIA

MOLDAVIA

BULGARIA

BYZANTINE EMPIRE

OTTOMAN TURKS

SELJUK TURKS

KINGDOM OF CYPRUS

KNIGHTS

DUCHY OF ATHENS

ACHAEA

PRIN. OF ALBANIA

GEORGIA

ARMENIA

EMP. OF TREBIZOND

DOMINIONS OF MOHAMMED ARTIN

KARA-KUYUNLI TURKOMENS

ARABIA

PRINCIPALITY OF MOSCOW

CRETE (To Venice)

CORSICA (To Genoa)

SARDINIA (To Aragon)

BALEARIC ISLANDS (To Aragon)

MALTA

RHODES (To Knights)

CHIOS

SHETLAND ISLANDS

ORKNEY ISLANDS

HEBRIDES

FAEROES

White Sea

Atlantic Ocean

North Sea

Baltic Sea

Mediterranean Sea

Black Sea

Caspian Sea

Adriatic Sea

Aegean Sea

Bay of Biscay

English Channel

Lake Ladoga

Moscow
Vladimir
Yaroslavl
Tula
Orel
Kazan
Bulgar
Novgorod
Smolensk
Minsk
Pinsk
Vitebsk
Vilna
Riga
Königsberg
Danzig
Warsaw
Lublin
Cracow
Gnesen
Posen
Kiev
Jassy
Kremnitz
Eger
Pest
Buda
Belgrade
Arad
Nissa
Sofia
Vidin
Bucharest
Varna
Nicopolis
Adrianople
Constantinople
Nicaea
Smyrna
Athens
Thessalonica
Ragusa
Durazzo
Taranto
Naples
Rome
Palermo
Messina
Reggio
Tunis
Algiers
Gibraltar
Cadiz
Seville
Cordova
Granada
Toledo
Salamanca
Leon
Santiago
Lisbon
Valencia
Saragossa
Barcelona
Bayonne
Bordeaux
Toulouse
Narbonne
Marseille
Avignon
Lyon
Limoges
Poitiers
Chinon
Nantes
Rennes
Caen
Harfleur
Rouen
Paris
Orleans
Troyes
Reims
Crecy
Calais
Brugs
Ghent
Agincourt
Bretigny
Vaucouleurs
Domremy
Compiegne
Dijon
Besançon
Basel
Strassburg
Constance
Munich
Regensburg
Salzburg
Vienna
Prague
Trier
Cologne
Mainz
Frankfurt
Magdeburg
Hamburg
Bremen
Lubeck
Stralsund
Copenhagen
Oslo
Bergen
Calmar
Stockholm
Upsala
Abo
Wisby
Pau
Pamplona
Milan
Turin
Genoa
Florence
Bologna
Ferrara
Trieste
Venice
Norwich
London
Lincoln
York
Chester
Berwick
Edinburgh
Carlisle
Aberdeen
Falkirk
Bannockburn
Dublin
Wexford
Cork
Armagh
Cherson
Azov (To Genoa)
Sarai
Astrakhan
Trebizond
Sinope
Tiflis
Tabriz
Mosul
Damascus
Tripoli
Antioch
Tarsus
Nicosia
Rhodes
Sardica

Tana
Tuis
Duro
Kuban

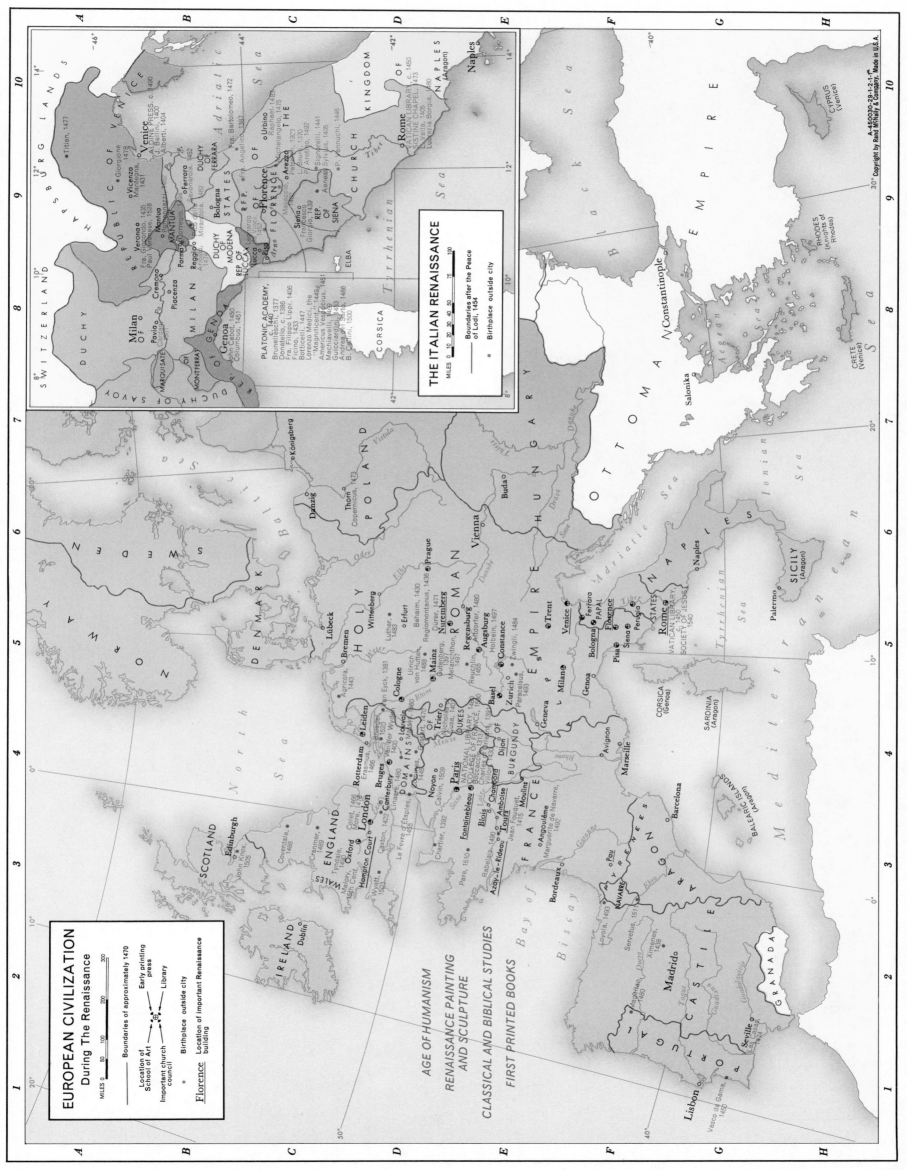

EUROPEAN CIVILIZATION
During The Renaissance

MILES 0   50   100   200   300

— Boundaries of approximately 1470
⊕ Location of School of Art
— Location of important church council
Florence Important Renaissance building
🖶 Early printing press
📖 Library
• Birthplace outside city
Florence Location of important Renaissance building

THE ITALIAN RENAISSANCE

MILES 0 10 20 30 40 50   100

— Boundaries after the Peace of Lodi, 1454
• Birthplace outside city

Inset map labels

HAPSBURG LANDS
SWITZERLAND
DUCHY OF MILAN
Milan
OF
Pavia
Cremona
Piacenza
Parma
REP. OF GENOA
Genoa
John Cabot
Columbus, 1451
MARQUISATE
MONTFERRAT
DUCHY OF SAVOY
REPUBLIC OF VENICE
Venice
ALDINE PRESS, c. 1490
J. Bellini, 1400
Alberti, 1404
Vicenza Mantegna, 1431
Verona
Mantua
Fra. Giocondo, 1435
Paul Veronese, 1528
Titian, 1477
Giorgione, 1478
DUCHY OF FERRARA
Ferrara
Regogio
DUCHY OF MODENA
REP. OF LUCCA
Lucca
Bologna
REP. OF FLORENCE
Florence
Savonarola, 1452
Pisa
Siena
REP. OF SIENA
Arezzo
Urbino
THE CHURCH STATES
Rome
Fra. Bartolomeo, 1472
Fra. Angelico, 1387
Raphael, 1483
Michelangelo, 1475
L. Valla, 1405
Lucrezia Borgia, 1480
NAPLES
Naples

PLATONIC ACADEMY, c. 1440
Brunelleschi, 1377
Donatello, c. 1386
Fra. Filippo Lippi, 1406
Ficino, 1433
Botticelli, 1447
Lorenzo Medici, the Magnificent, 1449
Americus Vespucius, 1451
Machiavelli, 1469
Guicciardini, 1483
Andrea del Sarto, 1486
B. Cellini, 1500

CORSICA
ELBA
Adriatic Sea
Tyrrhenian Sea

Main map labels

SWEDEN
NORWAY
SCOTLAND
Edinburgh
Coverdale, 1488
John Knox, 1505
IRELAND
Dublin
WALES
ENGLAND
London
Oxford
Canterbury
Hampton Court
Cranmer, 1489
Colet, 1466
More, 1478
Tyndale, 1492
Caxton, 1422
Wyatt, 1503
DENMARK
North Sea
Baltic Sea
Lübeck
Bremen
Danzig
Thorn Copernicus, 1473
POLAND
Königsberg
HOLY ROMAN EMPIRE
Wittenberg
Luther, 1483
Erfurt
Agricola, 1443
Cologne
Van Eyck, 1385
Mainz
Gutenberg, 1397
Leiden
Rotterdam
Erasmus, 1466
Bruges
Louvain
DOMAINS OF DUKES OF BURGUNDY
Brussels
Van der Weyden, 1400
Trier
Ulrich von Hutten, 1488
Regiomontanus, 1436
Dürer, 1471
Nuremberg
Behaim, 1430
Prague
Vienna
Budapest
HUNGARY
Regensburg
Augsburg
Reuchlin, 1455
Melanchthon, 1497
Holbein, 1497
Basel
Zurich
Zwingli, 1484
Constance
Paracelsus, 1493
Geneva
Calvin, 1509
FRANCE
Paris
COLLEGE OF FRANCE, 1530
NATIONAL LIBRARY
Rabelais, 1490
Budé, 1467
Boccaccio, 1313
Villon, 1431
Noyon
Fontainebleau
Blois
Amboise
Chambord
Tours
Jean Fouquet, 1415
Moulins
Dijon
Chartier, 1392
Le Fevre d'Etaples, 1455
Angoulême
Marguerite de Navarre, 1492
Loyola, 1493
Servetus, 1511
Ximenes, 1436
NAVARRE
Pau
ARAGON
Barcelona
NAVARRE, 1493
Bordeaux
PYRENEES
CASTILE
Madrid
PORTUGAL
Lisbon
Vasco da Gama, 1450
Magellan, 1480
Seville
Las Casas, 1474
GRANADA
Mediterranean Sea
CORSICA (Genoa)
SARDINIA (Aragon)
BALEARIC ISLANDS (Aragon)
Marseille
Avignon
SWITZERLAND
Milan
Genoa
Trent
Venice
PAPAL STATES
Ferrara
Bologna
Florence
Pisa
Siena
Perugia
VATICAN LIBRARY, c. 1450
SOCIETY OF JESUS, 1540
Rome
NAPLES
Naples
SICILY (Aragon)
Palermo
Tyrrhenian Sea
Adriatic Sea
Ionian Sea
Aegean Sea
OTTOMAN EMPIRE
Constantinople
Salonika
Black Sea
CRETE (Venice)
RHODES (Knights of Rhodes)
CYPRUS (Venice)
Bay of Biscay

AGE OF HUMANISM
RENAISSANCE PAINTING AND SCULPTURE
CLASSICAL AND BIBLICAL STUDIES
FIRST PRINTED BOOKS

A-450030-29-1-2-1-™
Copyright by Rand McNally & Company. Made in U.S.A.

13

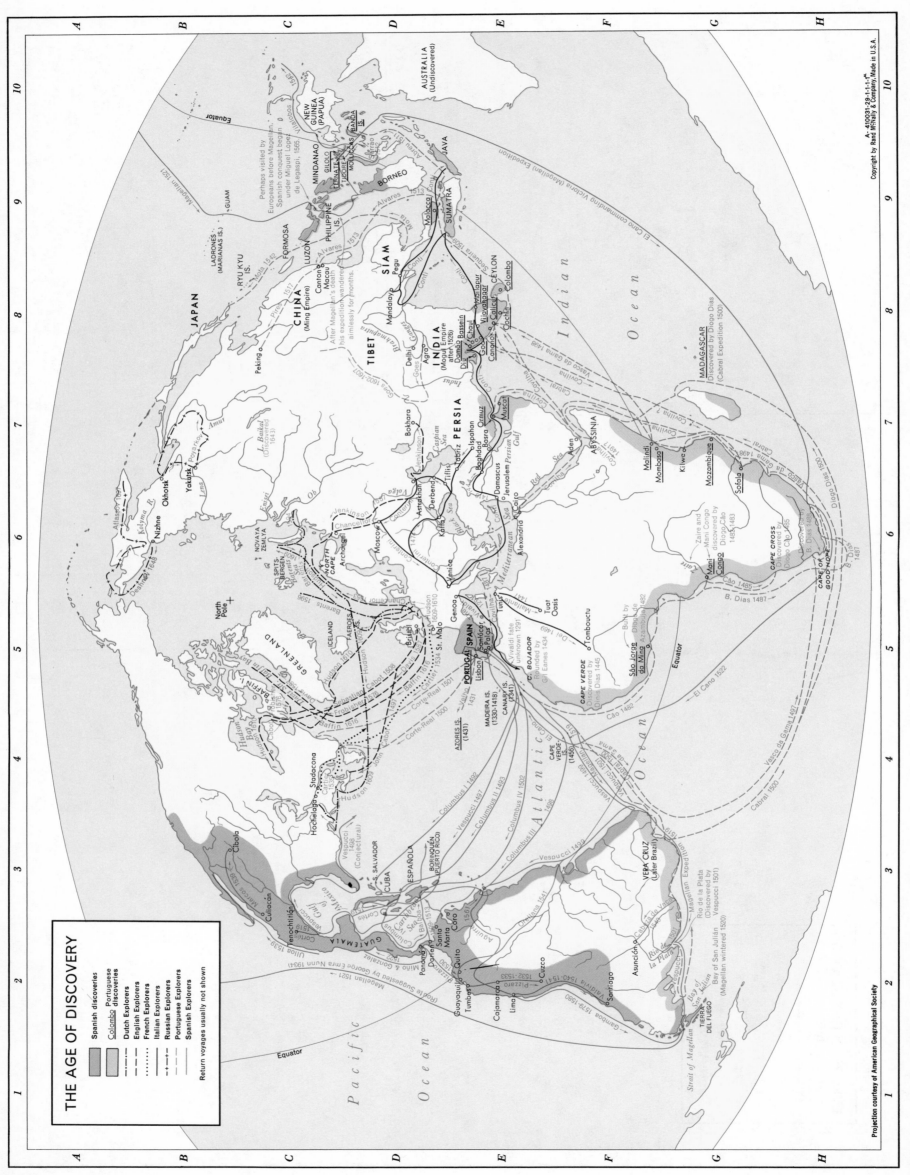

THE AGE OF DISCOVERY

Spanish discoveries
Portuguese discoveries
Colombo discoveries

- – - – - Dutch Explorers
- · · · · · English Explorers
- · · · · · French Explorers
- · · · · · Italian Explorers
- + + + + Russian Explorers
- – – – Portuguese Explorers
- – · · – Spanish Explorers
Return voyages usually not shown

A-410031-29-1-1-1-4™
Copyright by Rand McNally & Company, Made in U.S.A.
Projection courtesy of American Geographical Society

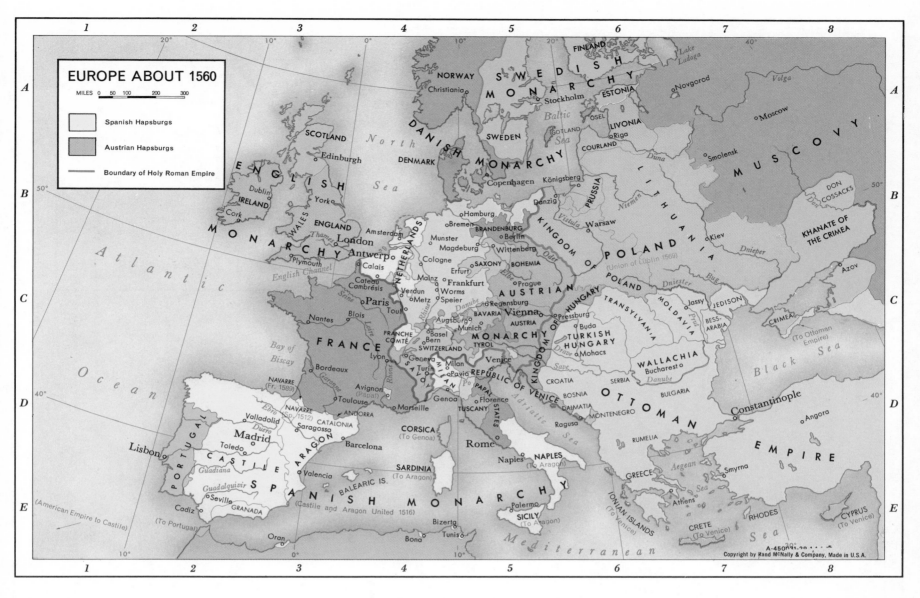

EUROPE ABOUT 1560

MILES 0 50 100 200 300

Spanish Hapsburgs

Austrian Hapsburgs

Boundary of Holy Roman Empire

NORWAY · Christiania

SWEDISH MONARCHY

FINLAND

DANISH MONARCHY

SWEDEN · Stockholm

Lake Ladoga · Volga

ESTONIA

OSEL

Baltic Sea

GOTLAND Sea

LIVONIA

COURLAND · Riga

Dvina

Novgorod

Moscow

MUSCOVY

SCOTLAND · Edinburgh

North Sea

DENMARK · Copenhagen

Königsberg

PRUSSIA · Danzig

Niemen

LITHUANIA

Smolensk

Dnieper

KHANATE OF THE CRIMEA

ENGLISH MONARCHY

WALES ENGLAND · York

IRELAND · Dublin

Cork

Amsterdam

NETHERLANDS

Hamburg · Bremen

BRANDENBURG · Berlin

Magdeburg

Wittenberg

Oder

KINGDOM OF POLAND

Warsaw

(Union of Lublin 1569)

Kiev

Azov

DON COSSACKS

Don

London · Antwerp

Plymouth · Calais

English Channel · Cateau Cambrésis

Cologne · SAXONY · BOHEMIA

Mainz · Erfurt · Frankfurt · Prague

POLAND

Dniester

Bug

MOLDAVIA · Jassy

JEDISON

CRIMEA (To Ottoman Empire)

Atlantic Ocean

Seine

Verdun · Metz · Speier

Worms · Toul

Regensburg

AUSTRIAN HUNGARY

TRANSYLVANIA

BESS-ARABIA

Paris · Blois

Rhine

Augsburg · Munich

BAVARIA

Vienna · AUSTRIA · Pressburg

Buda

TURKISH HUNGARY

Black Sea

Nantes · FRANCE

Loire · Lyon

FRANCHE COMTÉ

Basel · Bern

SWITZERLAND · Geneva

TYROL

Mohacs

WALLACHIA · Bucharest

Bordeaux

Garonne

NAVARRE (Fr. 1589)

Avignon (Papal)

Toulouse

ANDORRA

Rhône

Turin

SAVOY · Milan

Pavia

Po

Genoa

KINGDOM OF HUNGARY

REPUBLIC OF VENICE

Venice

CROATIA

BOSNIA

SERBIA · Danube

DALMATIA · Ragusa

MONTENEGRO

BULGARIA

OTTOMAN

Constantinople

Angora

Bay of Biscay

NAVARRE (Sp. 1512)

Ebro

Saragossa

ARAGON

Barcelona

CATALONIA

Marseille

PAPAL STATES · Florence

TUSCANY

Rome

EMPIRE

RUMELIA

GREECE

PORTUGAL

Lisbon

Valladolid

Duero

Guadiana

Madrid

Toledo

CASTILE

Valencia

BALEARIC IS.

CORSICA (To Genoa)

SARDINIA (To Aragon)

Naples · NAPLES (To Aragon)

MONTENEGRO

Aegean Sea

Smyrna

RHODES

Athens

CYPRUS (To Venice)

(American Empire to Castile)

Cadiz · Seville · GRANADA

SPANISH MONARCHY

(Castile and Aragon United 1516)

Oran

Bizerta

Bona · Tunis

Palermo

SICILY (To Aragon)

IONIAN ISLANDS (To Venice)

CRETE (To Venice)

Mediterranean

Copyright by Rand McNally & Company, Made in U.S.A.

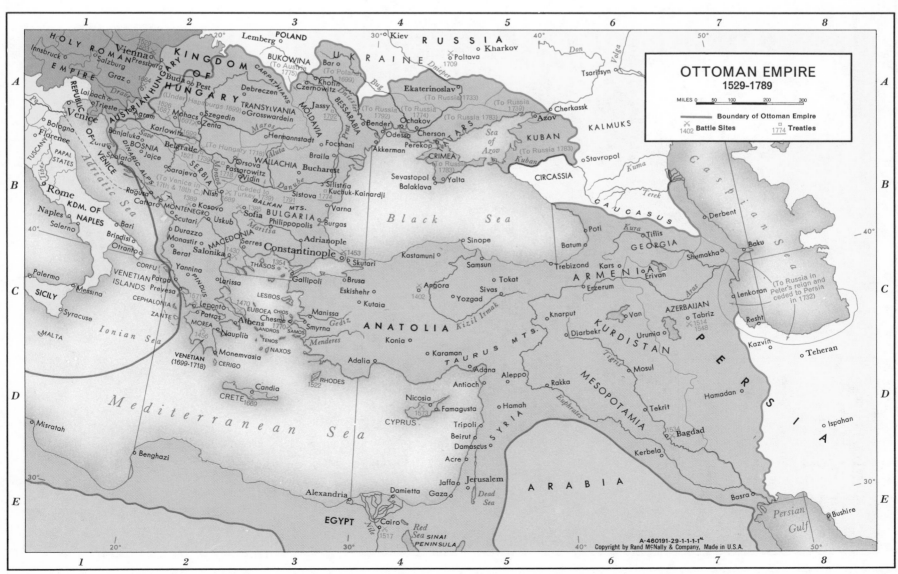

OTTOMAN EMPIRE
1529-1789

MILES 0 50 100 200 300

Boundary of Ottoman Empire

1402 Battle Sites

1774 Treaties

HOLY ROMAN EMPIRE

Innsbruck · Salzburg · Vienna

Graz

Laibach · AUSTRIAN HUNGARY

KINGDOM OF HUNGARY

POLAND · Lemberg

BUKOWINA (To Austria 1775)

CARPATHIANS

UKRAINE

Kiev

Poltava 1709

RUSSIA

Kharkov

Don

Tsaritsyn

Volga

REPUBLIC OF VENICE

Trieste · Agram

Buda · Pest

Debreczen

Szegedin

TRANSYLVANIA

Grosswardein

Czernowitz

Khotin

MOLDAVIA · Jassy

BESSARABIA

Ekaterinoslav (To Russia 1793)

Ochakov (To Russia 1792)

Odessa (To Russia 1791)

Bender

(To Poland 1699)

(To Russia 1774)

Cherkassk

Azov

KALMUKS

Bologna · Florence

TUSCANY

PAPAL STATES

Venice

ADRIATIC ALPS

Banjaluka

BOSNIA · Jajce

Karlowitz

Save

Belgrade

SERBIA

Akkerman

WALLACHIA · Bucharest

Braila

Perekop

CRIMEA (To Russia 1783)

Sea of Azov

Kuban (To Russia 1783)

KUBAN

Stavropol

Kuma

CIRCASSIA

Tiber · Rome

KDM. OF NAPLES

Naples · Bari

Ragusa

Cattaro

MONTENEGRO

Durazzo · Scutari

Uskub · Nish

Sofia

Philippopolis

BULGARIA

Silistria

Sistova 1791

Rustchuk 1774

Varna

Burgas

Sevastopol

Balaklava

Yalta

Black Sea

Poti

Terek

CAUCASUS

Batum

GEORGIA

Tiflis

Shemakha

Derbent

Caspian Sea

Baku

Salerno · Brindisi · Otranto

Durazzo

MACEDONIA

Serres · Salonika

Constantinople 1453

Skutari

Kastamuni

Sinope

Samsun

Trebizond

Kars

Erzerum

ARMENIA

Erivan

(To Russia in Peter's reign and ceded to Persia in 1732)

CORFU

VENETIAN ISLANDS

Parga · Prevesa 1571

PINDUS

Yannina

Larissa

THASOS

LESBOS

EUBOEA CHIOS

Chesme 1770

Brusa

Eskishehr

Kutaia

ANATOLIA

Angora 1402

Tokat

Sivas

Yozgad

Kizil Irmak

Erzerum

Van

Knarput

AZERBAIJAN · Tabriz 1514 1548

Lenkoran

KURDISTAN

Diarbekr

Urumia

Resht

Kazvin

CEPHALONIA

ZANTE

MOREA

Lepanto · Patras 1470

Athens 1456

Nauplia

SAMOS

Smyrna

Manissa

Gediz

Menderes

Konia

KARAMAN

Adalia

TAURUS MTS.

Adana

Aleppo

Mosul

Tigris

Bagdad 1534

Teheran

PERSIA

Ispahan

MALTA

Ionian Sea

VENETIAN (1699-1718)

CERIGO

NAXOS

TENOS

Monemvasia

Naxos

RHODES 1522

CRETE · Candia 1669

CYPRUS

Nicosia

Famagusta

Antioch

Hamah

Rakka

MESOPOTAMIA

Tekrit

Hamadan

Kerbela

Basra

Bushire

Persian Gulf

Misratah

Benghazi

Mediterranean Sea

Alexandria

Damietta · Gaza

Jaffa · Jerusalem

Dead Sea

Tripoli · Beirut

Damascus · Acre

SYRIA

ARABIA

EGYPT · Cairo 1517

Nile

Red Sea

SINAI PENINSULA

Copyright by Rand McNally & Company, Made in U.S.A.

15

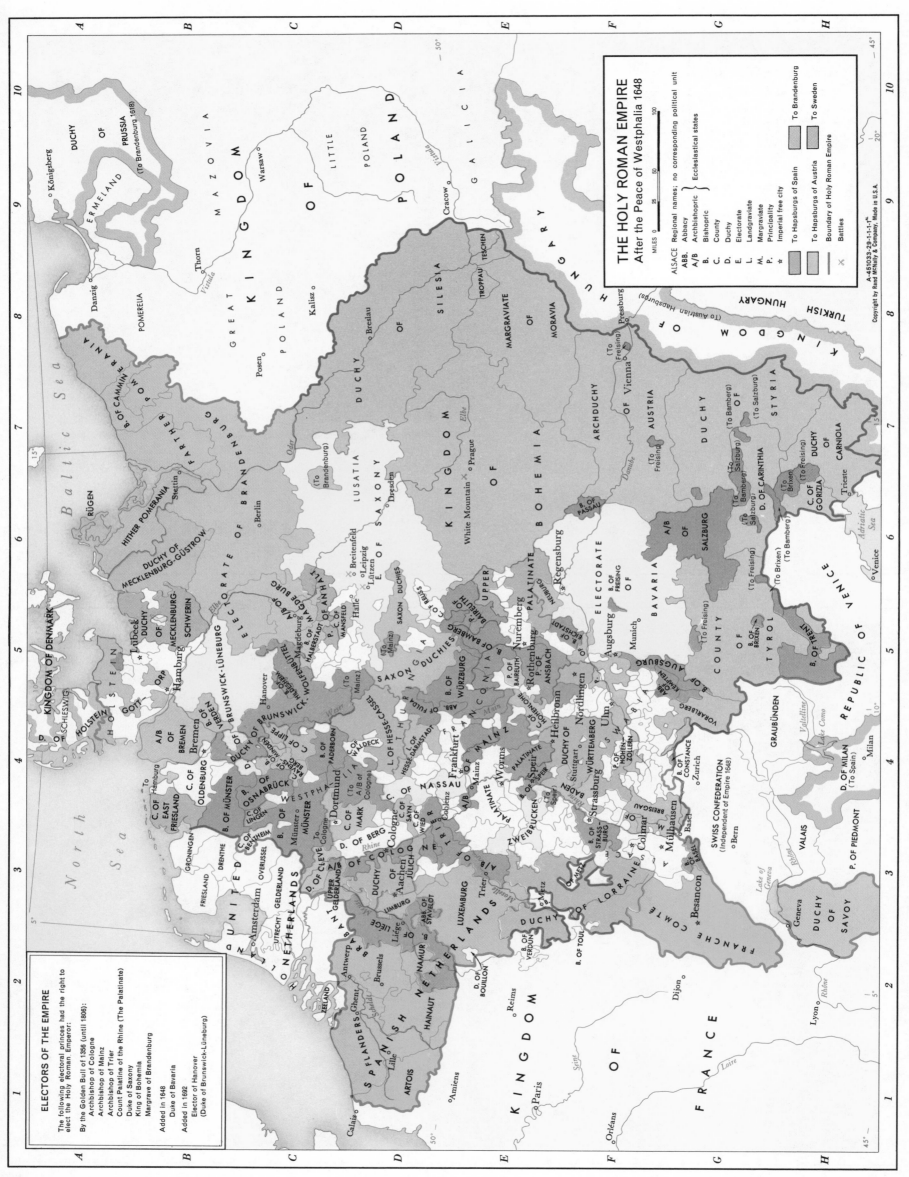

THE HOLY ROMAN EMPIRE
After the Peace of Westphalia 1648

MILES 0   25   50   100

ALSACE Regional names; no corresponding political unit

ABB.	Abbacy	} Ecclesiastical states
A/B	Archbishopric	
B.	Bishopric	
C.	County	
D.	Duchy	
E.	Electorate	
L.	Landgraviate	
M.	Margraviate	
P.	Principality	
★	Imperial free city	

To Brandenburg
To Sweden
To Hapsburgs of Spain
To Hapsburgs of Austria
Boundary of Holy Roman Empire
× Battles

A-451033-29-1-1-1-4L

Copyright by Rand McNally & Company. Made in U.S.A.

ELECTORS OF THE EMPIRE

The following electoral princes had the right to elect the Holy Roman Emperor:

By the Golden Bull of 1356 (until 1806):
Archbishop of Cologne
Archbishop of Mainz
Archbishop of Trier
Count Palatine of the Rhine (The Palatinate)
Duke of Saxony
King of Bohemia
Margrave of Brandenburg

Added in 1648
Duke of Bavaria

Added in 1692
Elector of Hanover
(Duke of Brunswick-Lüneburg)

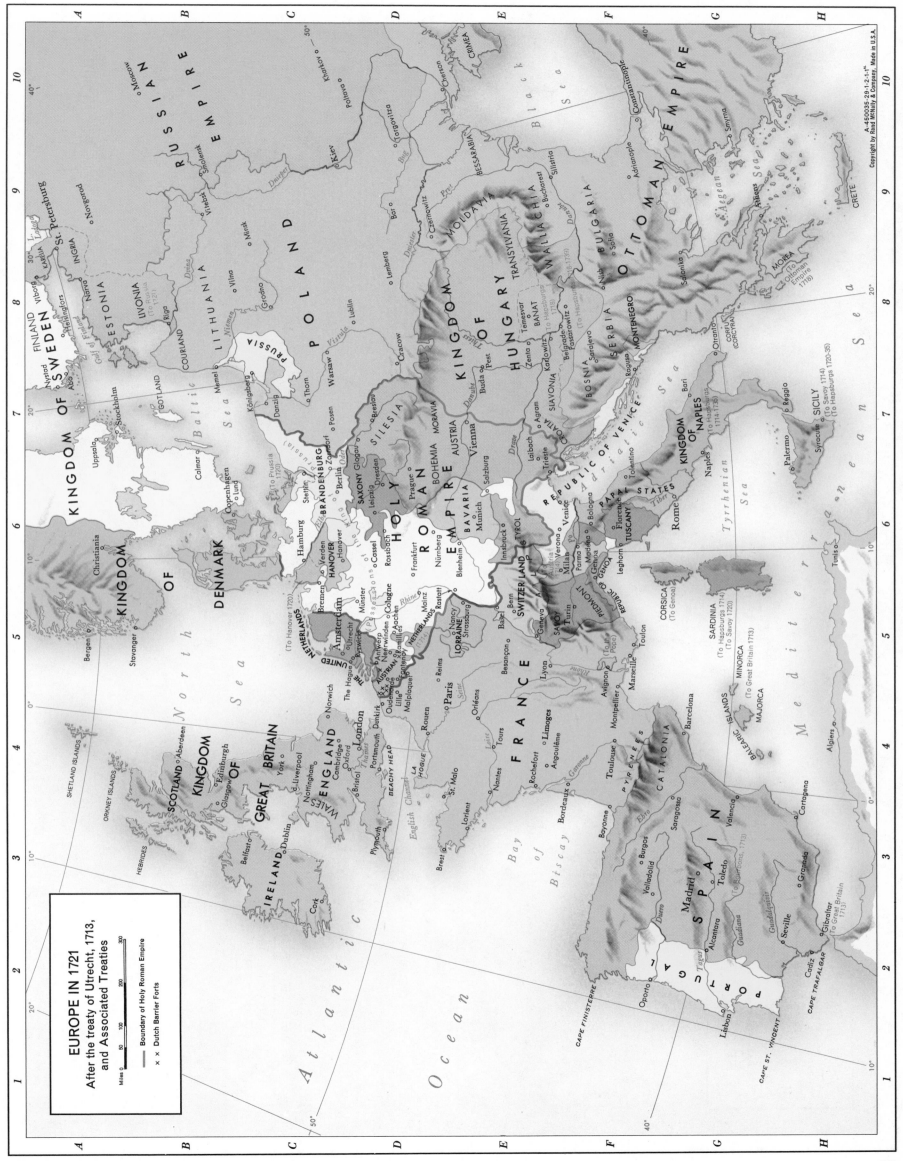

EUROPE IN 1721

After the treaty of Utrecht, 1713, and Associated Treaties

Miles 0 50 100 200 300

——— Boundary of Holy Roman Empire
× × Dutch Barrier Forts

17

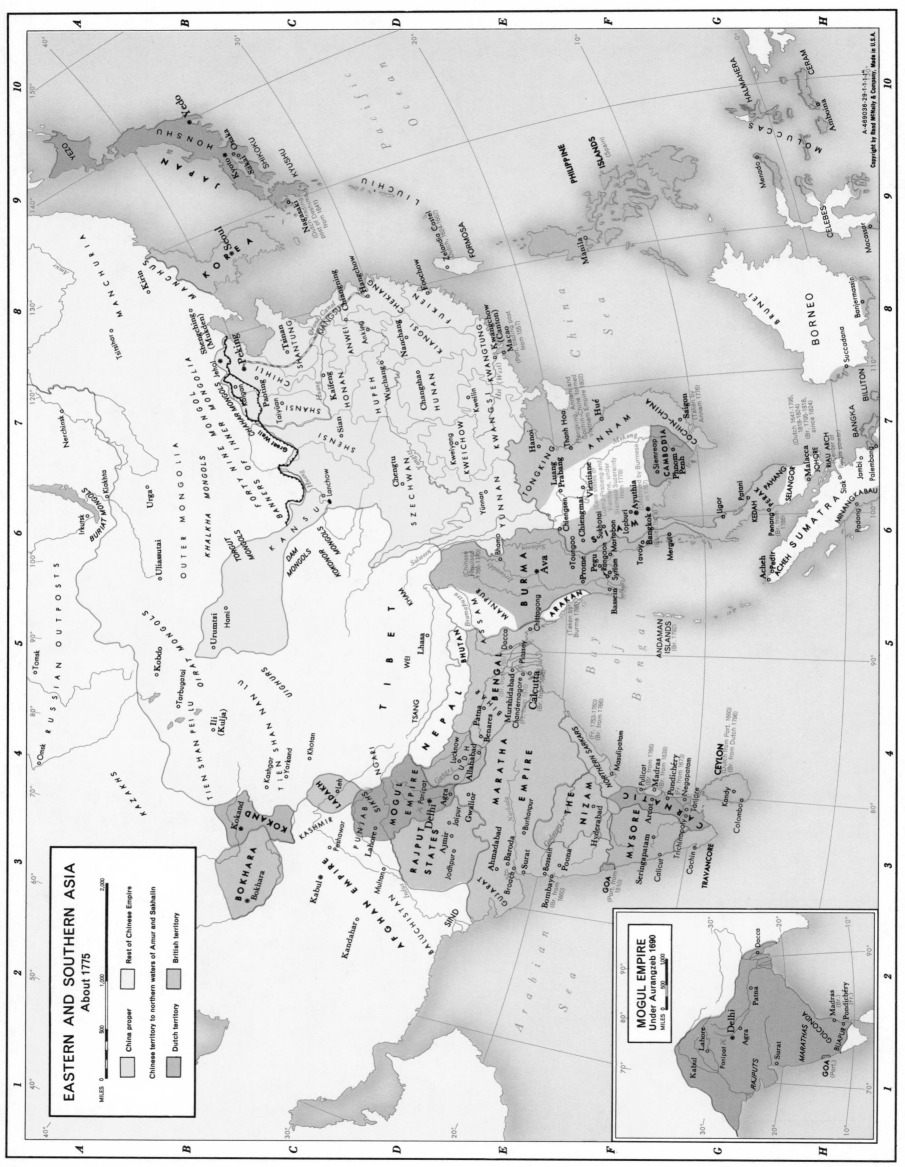

EASTERN AND SOUTHERN ASIA
About 1775

MILES 0   500   1,000   2,000

- China proper
- Rest of Chinese Empire
- Chinese territory to northern waters of Amur and Sakhalin
- Dutch territory
- British territory

MOGUL EMPIRE
Under Aurangzeb 1690

MILES 0   500   1000

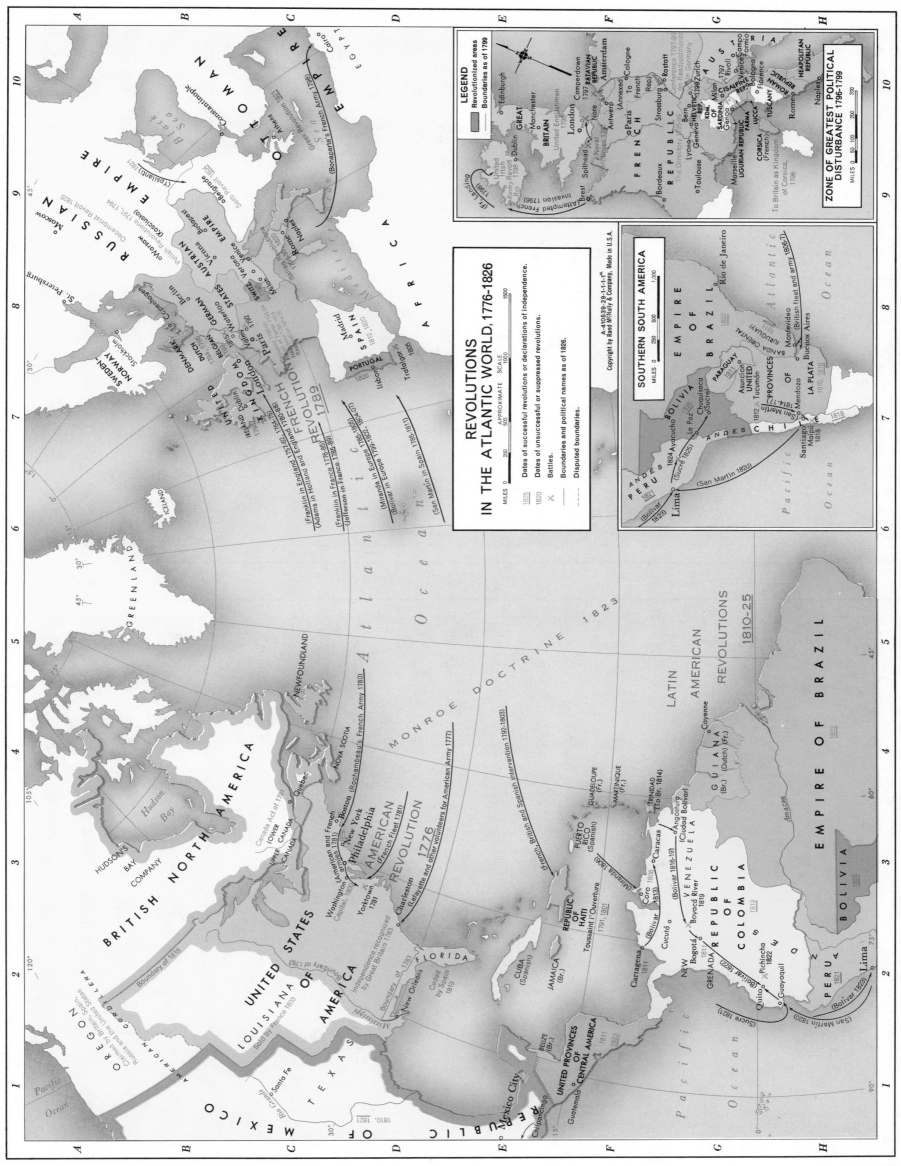

REVOLUTIONS IN THE ATLANTIC WORLD, 1776-1826

LEGEND

Revolutionized areas

Boundaries as of 1799

ZONE OF GREATEST POLITICAL DISTURBANCE 1796-1799

MILES 0 50 100 200 300

SOUTHERN SOUTH AMERICA

MILES 0 250 500 1,000

A-410539-29-1-1-1-1 Made in U.S.A.
Copyright by Rand McNally & Company.

1825 Dates of successful revolutions or declarations of independence.

1820 Dates of unsuccessful or suppressed revolutions.

X Battles.

Boundaries and political names as of 1826.

------ Disputed boundaries.

MILES 0 250 500 1000 1500
APPROXIMATE SCALE

BRITISH NORTH AMERICA

UNITED STATES OF AMERICA

AMERICAN REVOLUTION 1776

FRENCH REVOLUTION 1789

EMPIRE OF BRAZIL

REPUBLIC OF COLOMBIA

LATIN AMERICAN REVOLUTIONS 1810-25

MONROE DOCTRINE 1823

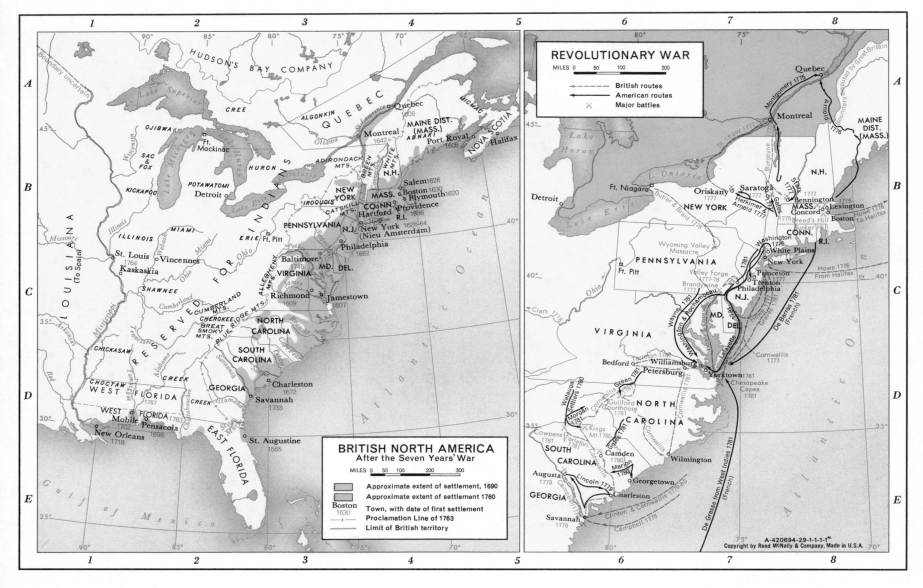

REVOLUTIONARY WAR

MILES 0 50 100 200

←—→ British routes
←— American routes
× Major battles

BRITISH NORTH AMERICA
After the Seven Years' War

MILES 0 50 100 200 300

Approximate extent of settlement, 1690
Approximate extent of settlement 1760
Boston 1630 Town, with date of first settlement
Proclamation Line of 1763
Limit of British territory

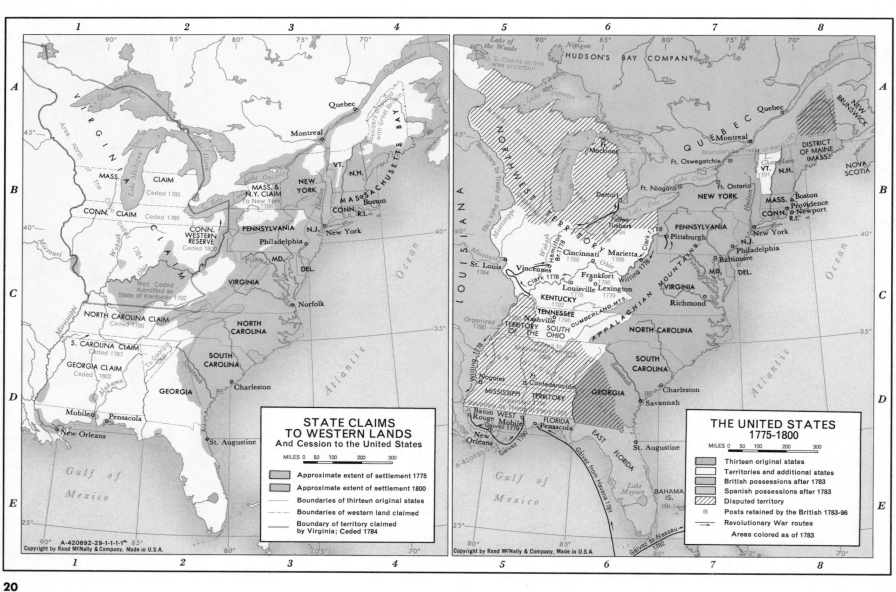

STATE CLAIMS TO WESTERN LANDS
And Cession to the United States

MILES 0 50 100 200 300

Approximate extent of settlement 1775
Approximate extent of settlement 1800
Boundaries of thirteen original states
Boundaries of western land claimed
Boundary of territory claimed by Virginia; Ceded 1784

THE UNITED STATES
1775–1800

MILES 0 50 100 200 300

Thirteen original states
Territories and additional states
British possessions after 1783
Spanish possessions after 1783
Disputed territory
Posts retained by the British 1783–96
Revolutionary War routes
Areas colored as of 1783

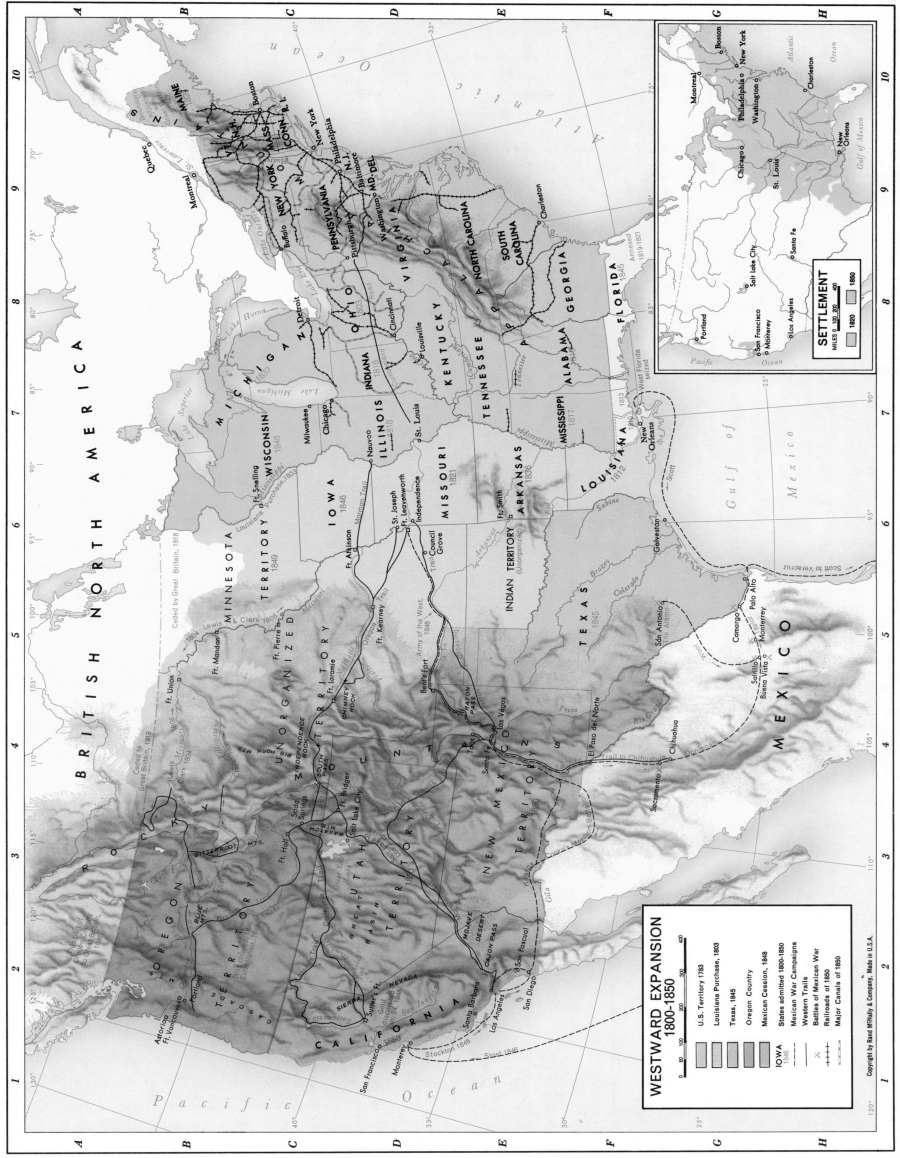

WESTWARD EXPANSION
1800-1850

U.S. Territory 1783
Louisiana Purchase, 1803
Texas, 1845
Oregon Country
Mexican Cession, 1848
States admitted 1800-1850
IOWA 1846
Mexican War Campaigns
Western Trails
Battles of Mexican War
Railroads of 1850
Major Canals of 1850

SETTLEMENT
MILES 0 100 200 400
1820
1850

Copyright by Rand McNally & Company, Made in U.S.A.

21

LATIN AMERICA ABOUT 1790

MILES 0   250   500   1,000

European Colonies

Spain
Great Britain
Netherlands
Portugal
France
Seat of Government

1535 Lima Dates indicate year of founding

BRITISH NORTH AMERICA

UNITED STATES OF AMERICA

CAPTAINCY-GENERAL OF LOUISIANA

INTENDANCY OF NUEVA CALIFORNIA
San Francisco 1776
Monterey 1770
San Luis Obispo 1772
Santa Barbara
San Juan
Los Angeles 1781
San Diego 1769
La Paz 1535
VICEROYALTY OF VIEJA CALIFORNIA
INTENDANCY OF NEW SPAIN
WESTERN INTERIOR PROVINCES
EASTERN INTERIOR PROVINCES
INTENDANCY OF NUEVO MEXICO
Santa Fé
El Paso
PRESIDENCY
INTENDANCY OF SONORA (AUDIENCIA)
Chihuahua
INTENDANCY OF DURANGO
INTENDANCY OF GUADALAJARA
Laredo 1775
Saltillo
San Antonio 1718
St. Louis 1764
Culiacán 1531
INTENDANCY OF ZACATECAS
San Luis Potosí
Querétaro 1550
INTENDANCY OF VALLADOLID
Mexico City 1521
INTENDANCY OF MEXICO
Vera Cruz 1519
INTENDANCY OF YUCATAN
INTENDANCY OF OAXACA
CHIAPAS
Belice
CAPTAINCY-GENERAL (AUDIENCIA) OF GUATEMALA
Guatemala
San Salvador 1525
León
Granada 1524
San José 1738
Cartago 1564
Portobelo 1584
Panama 1519

New Orleans 1718
Pensacola 1698
WEST FLORIDA
EAST FLORIDA
St. Augustine 1565
Disputed with U.S. 1783-1795

Habana 1515
CAPTAINCY-GENERAL OF CUBA
Santiago 1514
JAMAICA Br. 1655
Port au Prince 1749
Santo Domingo 1496
San Juan 1511
PUERTO RICO
CAPTAINCY-GENERAL OF SANTO DOMINGO Ceded to France 1795

Gulf of Mexico
Caribbean Sea
Atlantic Ocean
Tropic of Cancer

Santa Marta 1525
Cartagena 1533
La Guaira 1589
Caracas 1567
TRINIDAD Ceded to Great Britain, 1802
CAPTAINCY-GENERAL OF CARACAS
VICEROYALTY OF NEW GRANADA Established 1717, Restored 1740
Bogotá
SANTA FÉ

Stabroek (Georgetown) Approx. 1740
Paramaribo 1640
Cayenne 1664
DUTCH GUIANA Dutch in 1790
FRENCH GUIANA

GALAPAGOS IS. Claimed by Spain, but unoccupied

Quito 1534
PRESIDENCY (AUDIENCIA) OF QUITO
Guayaquil 1535
AUDIENCIA OF LIMA
VICEROYALTY OF PERU
Trujillo 1535
Callao 1537
Lima 1535
Cuzco 1533
PRESIDENCY (AUDIENCIA) OF CUZCO
PRESIDENCY (AUDIENCIA) OF CHARCAS
La Paz
Chuquisaca 1538
Potosí 1545

Barcelos 1658
CAPTAINCY OF RIO NEGRO
Barra do Rio Negro 1660
Tabatinga 1780
Belem 1616
São Luis 1612
CAPTAINCY OF PARÁ
CAPTAINCY OF MARANHÃO
Fortaleza 1609
CAPTAINCY OF PIAUI
Recife (Pernambuco) 1561
CAPTAINCY OF PERNAMBUCO
CAPTAINCY OF SERGIPE
CAPTAINCY OF BAÍA
Salvador (Baía) 1549
VICEROYALTY OF BRAZIL Definitively established 1714
Principe da Beira 1760
CAPTAINCY OF MATO GROSSO
Villa Bella (Mato Grosso) 1752
Santa Anna (Goiaz) 1736
Santa Anna (Goiaz)
CAPTAINCY OF GOIAZ
Tijuco (Diamantina)
MINAS GERAIS
Ouro Preto 1698
CAPTAINCY OF ESPIRITO SANTO
CAPTAINCY OF RIO DE JANEIRO
Rio de Janeiro 1567
Santos 1536
São Paulo
CAPTAINCY OF SÃO PAULO
CAPTAINCY OF SANTA CATARINA
CAPTAINCY OF RIO GRANDE DO SUL
Porto Alegre 1743
Rio Grande 1737

VICEROYALTY OF LA PLATA (Created 1776)
Salta
Tucumán 1586
PARAGUAY
Asunción 1537
São Paulo
La Serena 1544
Mendoza
Córdoba
Santa Fé 1573
BANDA ORIENTAL
Colonia
Valparaíso 1544
Santiago 1541
BUENOS AIRES
Buenos Aires 1580
Montevideo 1724
CAPTAINCY-GENERAL (AUDIENCIA) OF CHILE Loosely linked to Peru
AUDIENCIA OF Santa Fé
Concepción 1550
Valdivia 1552
CHILOE I.
PATAGONIA
TIERRA DEL FUEGO
CAPE HORN
MALVINAS (FALKLAND ISLANDS)
Drake Passage

Pacific Ocean
Tropic of Capricorn

A-440037-29-1-1-1-1
Copyright by Rand McNally & Company, Made in U.S.A.

22

LATIN AMERICA AFTER
INDEPENDENCE

MILES 0   250   500   1,000

23

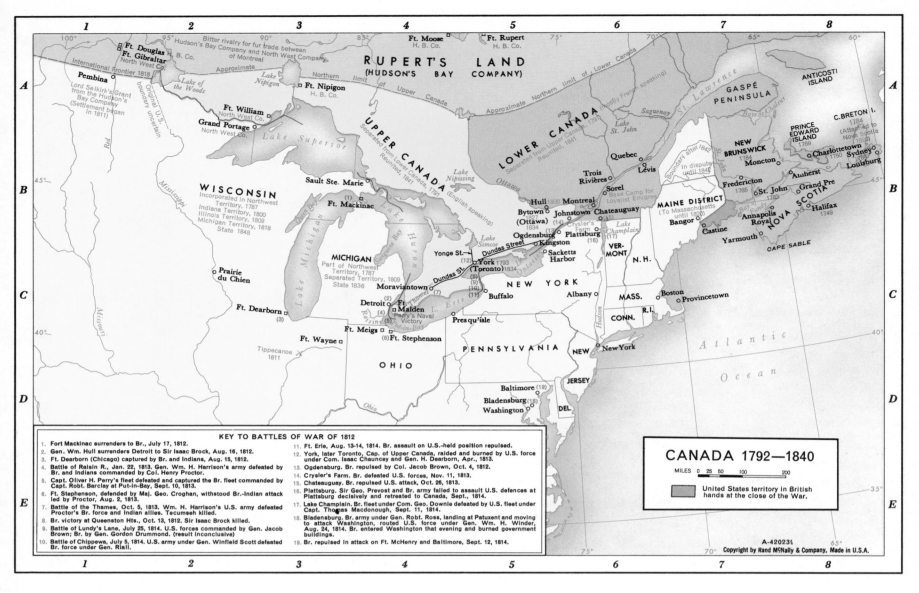

KEY TO BATTLES OF WAR OF 1812

1. Fort Mackinac surrenders to Br., July 17, 1812.
2. Gen. Wm. Hull surrenders Detroit to Sir Isaac Brock, Aug. 16, 1812.
3. Ft. Dearborn (Chicago) captured by Br. and Indians, Aug. 15, 1812.
4. Battle of Raisin R., Jan. 22, 1813. Gen. Wm. H. Harrison's army defeated by Br. and Indians commanded by Col. Henry Proctor.
5. Capt. Oliver H. Perry's fleet defeated and captured the Br. fleet commanded by Capt. Robt. Barclay at Put-in-Bay, Sept. 10, 1813.
6. Ft. Stephenson, defended by Maj. Geo. Croghan, withstood Br.-Indian attack led by Proctor, Aug. 2, 1813.
7. Battle of the Thames, Oct. 5, 1813. Wm. H. Harrison's U.S. army defeated Proctor's Br. force and Indian allies. Tecumseh killed.
8. Br. victory at Queenston Hts., Oct. 13, 1812. Sir Isaac Brock killed.
9. Battle of Lundy's Lane, July 25, 1814. U.S. forces commanded by Gen. Jacob Brown; Br. by Gen. Gordon Drummond. (result inconclusive)
10. Battle of Chippewa, July 5, 1814. U.S. army under Gen. Winfield Scott defeated Br. force under Gen. Riall.
11. Ft. Erie, Aug. 13-14, 1814. Br. assault on U.S.-held position repulsed.
12. York, later Toronto, Cap. of Upper Canada, raided and burned by U.S. force under Com. Isaac Chauncey and Gen. H. Dearborn, Apr., 1813.
13. Ogdensburg. Br. repulsed by Col. Jacob Brown, Oct. 4, 1812.
14. Crysler's Farm. Br. defeated U.S. forces, Nov. 11, 1813.
15. Chateauguay. Br. repulsed U.S. attack, Oct. 26, 1813.
16. Plattsburg. Sir Geo. Prevost and Br. army failed to assault U.S. defences at Plattsburg decisively and retreated to Canada, Sept., 1814.
17. Lake Champlain. Br. fleet under Com. Geo. Downie defeated by U.S. fleet under Capt. Thomas Macdonough, Sept. 11, 1814.
18. Bladensburg. Br. army under Gen. Robt. Ross, landing at Patuxent and moving to attack Washington, routed U.S. force under Gen. Wm. H. Winder, Aug. 24, 1814. Br. entered Washington that evening and burned government buildings.
19. Br. repulsed in attack on Ft. McHenry and Baltimore, Sept. 12, 1814.

CANADA 1792—1840

MILES 0 25 50 100 200

United States territory in British hands at the close of the War.

A-420239
Copyright by Rand McNally & Company, Made in U.S.A.

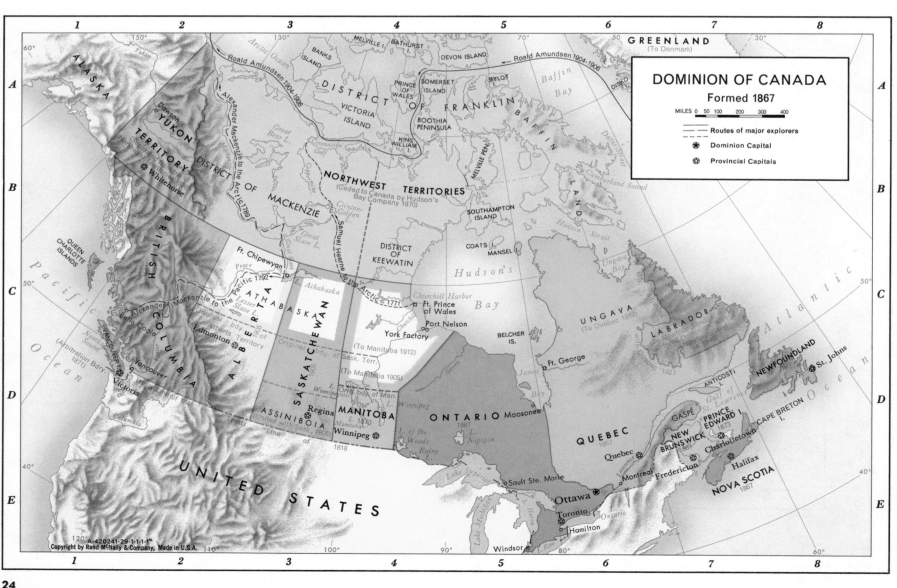

DOMINION OF CANADA
Formed 1867

MILES 0 50 100 200 300 400

--- Routes of major explorers
✳ Dominion Capital
✳ Provincial Capitals

A-420241-29-1-1-1
Copyright by Rand McNally & Company, Made in U.S.A.

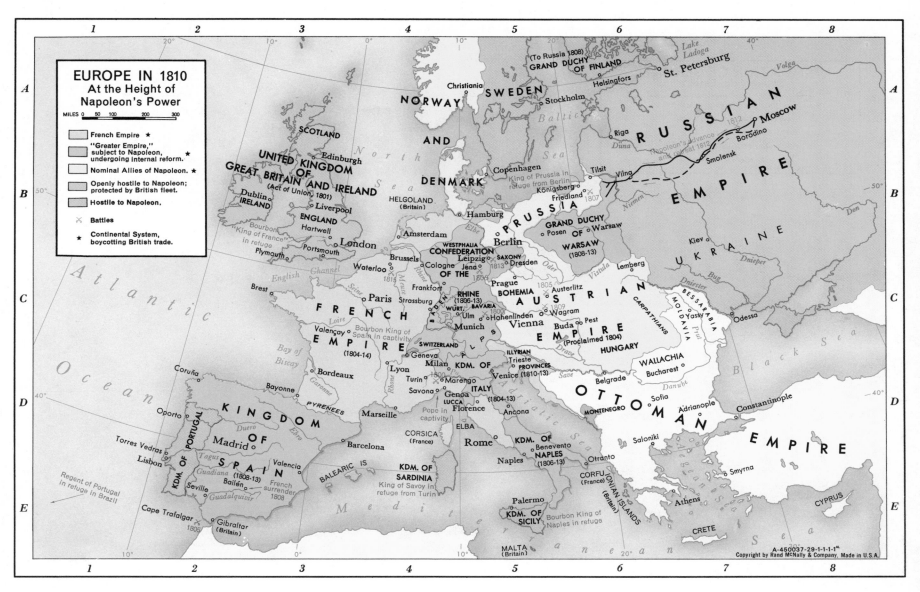

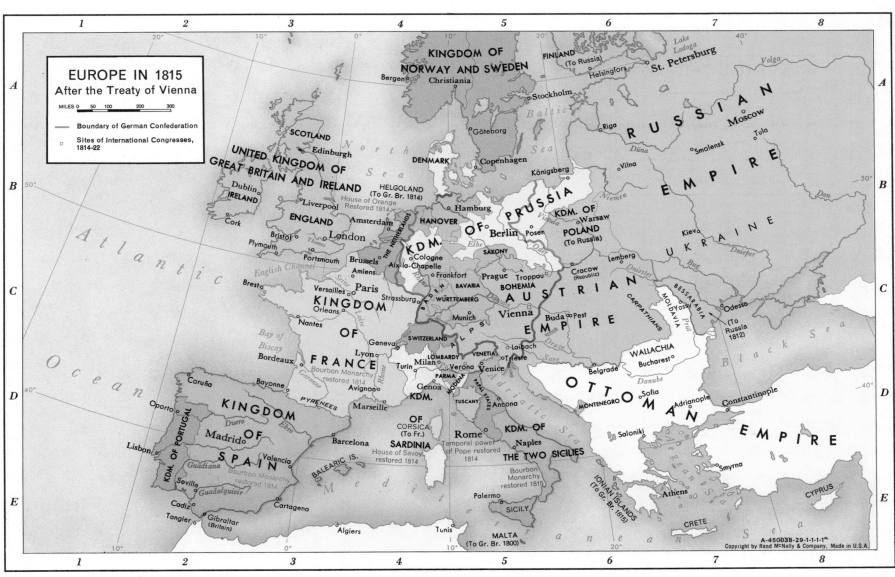

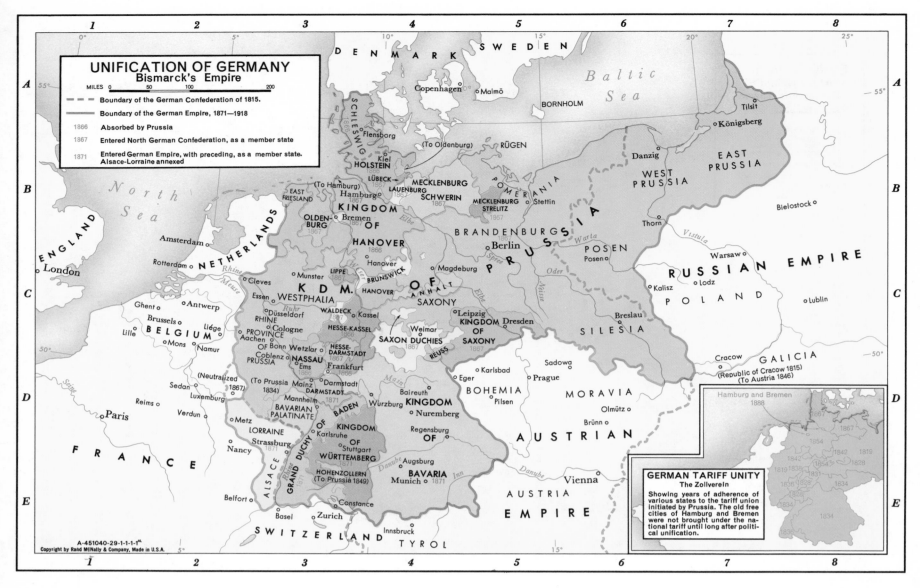

UNIFICATION OF GERMANY — Bismarck's Empire

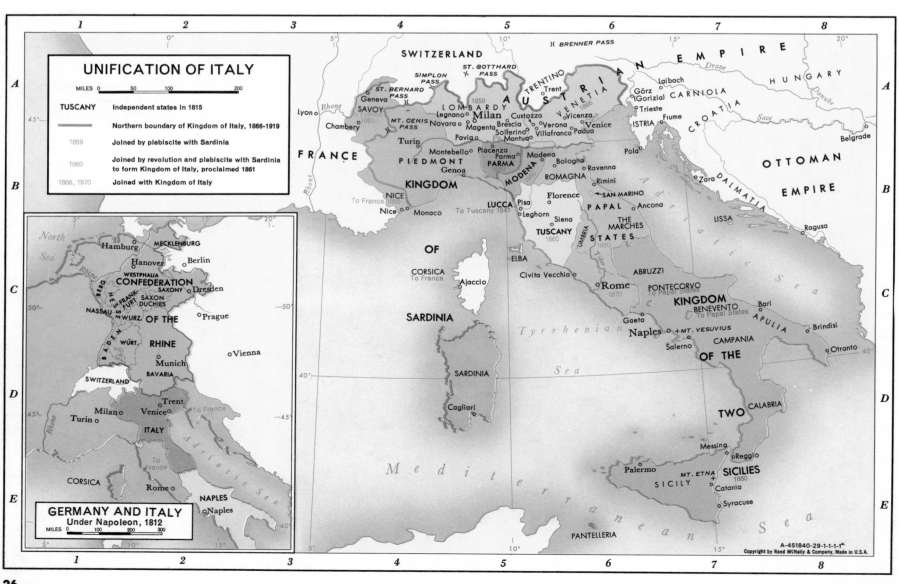

UNIFICATION OF ITALY

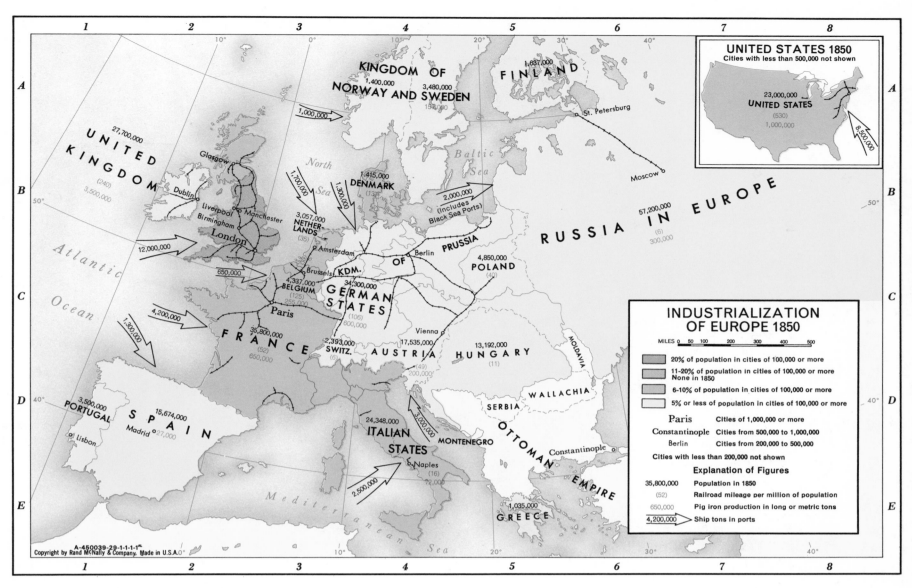

INDUSTRIALIZATION OF EUROPE 1850

MILES 0 50 100 200 300 400 500

- 20% of population in cities of 100,000 or more
- 11-20% of population in cities of 100,000 or more None in 1850
- 6-10% of population in cities of 100,000 or more
- 5% or less of population in cities of 100,000 or more

Paris — Cities of 1,000,000 or more
Constantinople — Cities from 500,000 to 1,000,000
Berlin — Cities from 200,000 to 500,000

Cities with less than 200,000 not shown

Explanation of Figures

35,800,000 — Population in 1850
(52) — Railroad mileage per million of population
650,000 — Pig iron production in long or metric tons
4,200,000 → Ship tons in ports

A-450039-29-1-1-1-1 ᴬᴸ
Copyright by Rand McNally & Company, Made in U.S.A.

UNITED STATES 1850
Cities with less than 500,000 not shown

23,000,000
UNITED STATES
(530)
1,000,000

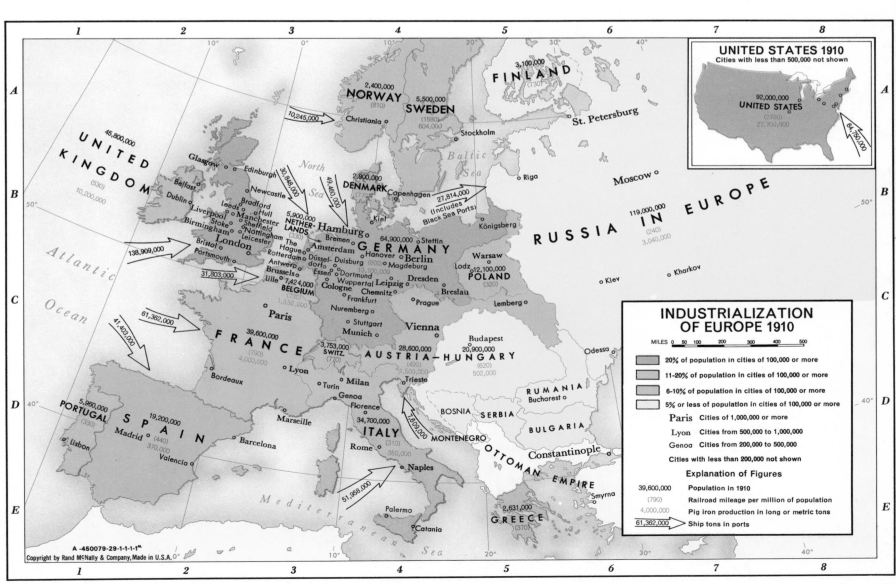

INDUSTRIALIZATION OF EUROPE 1910

MILES 0 50 100 200 300 400 500

- 20% of population in cities of 100,000 or more
- 11-20% of population in cities of 100,000 or more
- 6-10% of population in cities of 100,000 or more
- 5% or less of population in cities of 100,000 or more

Paris — Cities of 1,000,000 or more
Lyon — Cities from 500,000 to 1,000,000
Genoa — Cities from 200,000 to 500,000

Cities with less than 200,000 not shown

Explanation of Figures

39,600,000 — Population in 1910
(790) — Railroad mileage per million of population
4,000,000 — Pig iron production in long or metric tons
61,362,000 → Ship tons in ports

A-450079-29-1-1-1-1 ᴬᴸ
Copyright by Rand McNally & Company, Made in U.S.A.

UNITED STATES 1910
Cities with less than 500,000 not shown

92,000,000
UNITED STATES
(2720)
27,700,000

27

EXPANSION OF RUSSIA IN EUROPE

MILES 0 50 100   200   300   400

Russia 1533	Acquired to 1914
Acquired to 1598	Held at other times

Dates indicate time area held or gained by Russia.

A-470195-29-1-1-1-1
Copyright by Rand McNally & Company, Made in U.S.A.

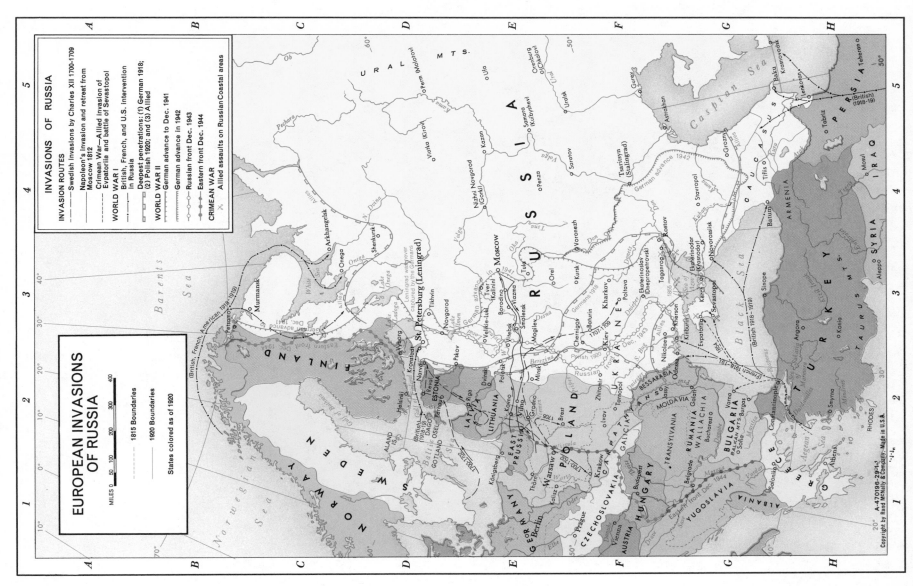

EUROPEAN INVASIONS OF RUSSIA

INVASIONS OF RUSSIA

INVASION ROUTES

Swedish invasions by Charles XII 1700-1709

Napoleon's invasion and retreat from Moscow 1812

Crimean War—Allied invasion of Evpatoria and battle of Sevastopol

WORLD WAR I

British, French, and U.S. Intervention in Russia

Deepest penetrations: (1) German 1918; (2) Polish 1920; and (3) Allied

WORLD WAR II

German advance to Dec. 1941

German advance in 1942

Russian front Dec. 1943

Eastern front Dec. 1944

CRIMEAN WAR

Allied assaults on Russian coastal areas

MILES 0 50 100 200 300 400

1815 Boundaries

1920 Boundaries

States colored as of 1920

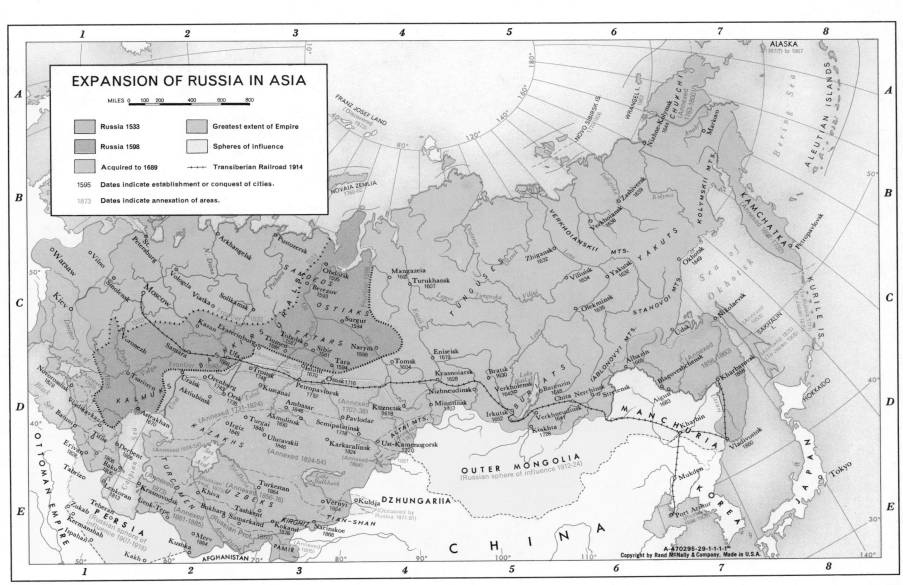

EXPANSION OF RUSSIA IN ASIA

MILES 0 100 200 400 600 800

Russia 1533

Russia 1598

Acquired to 1689

Greatest extent of Empire

Spheres of influence

Transiberian Railroad 1914

1595 — Dates indicate establishment or conquest of cities.

1873 — Dates indicate annexation of areas.

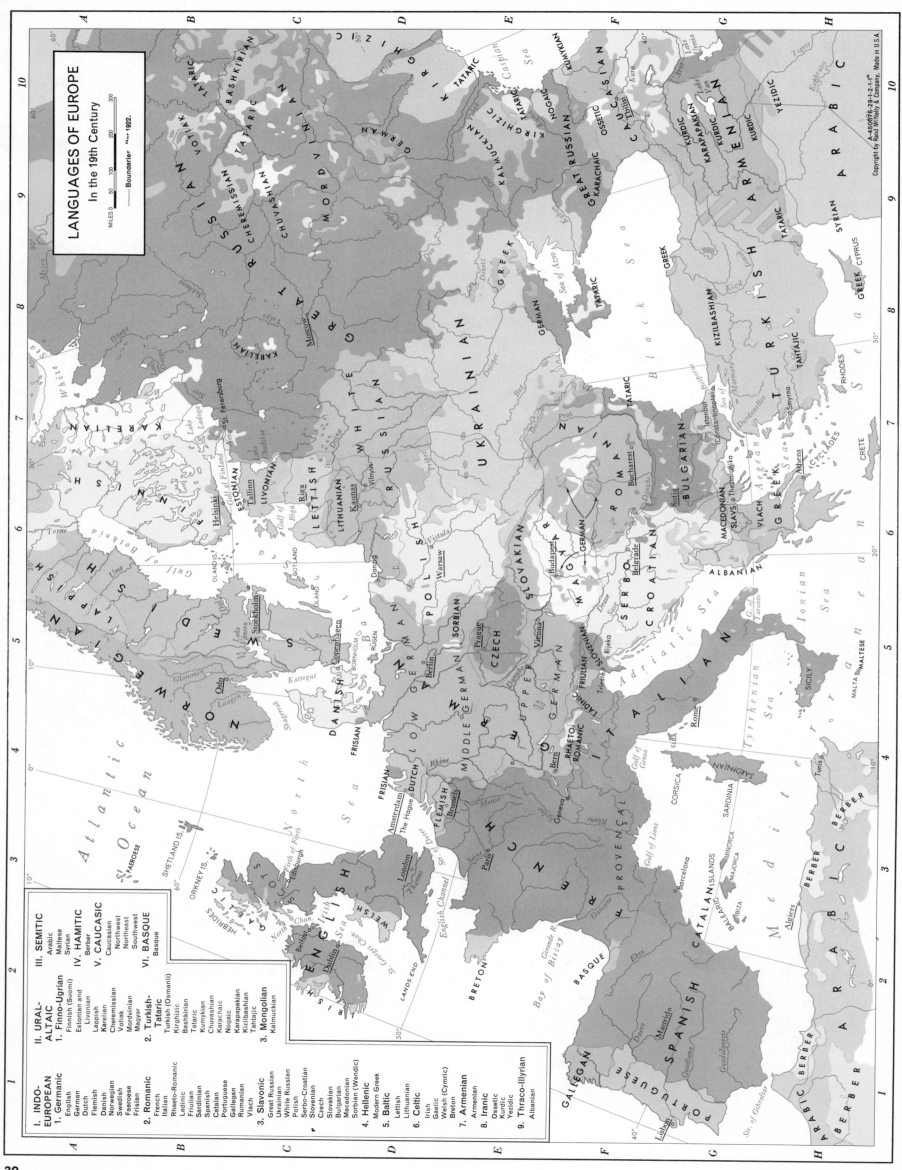

LANGUAGES OF EUROPE
In the 19th Century

MILES 0 50 100 200 300
———— Boundaries 1922.

Legend:

I. INDO-EUROPEAN
1. Germanic
English
German
Dutch
Flemish
Danish
Norwegian
Swedish
Faeroese
Frisian
2. Romanic
French
Italian
Rhaeto-Romanic
Ladinic
Friulian
Sardinian
Spanish
Catalan
Portuguese
Gallegan
Rumanian
Vlach
3. Slavonic
Great Russian
Ukrainian
White Russian
Polish
Czech
Slovakian
Bulgarian
Macedonian
Sorbian (Wendic)
4. Hellenic
Modern Greek
5. Baltic
Lettish
Lithuanian
6. Celtic
Irish
Gaelic
Welsh (Cymric)
Breton
7. Armenian
Armenian
8. Iranic
Ossetic
Kurdic
Yezidic
9. Thraco-Illyrian
Albanian

II. URAL-ALTAIC
1. Finno-Ugrian
Finnish (Suomi)
Estonian and Livonian
Lappish
Karelian
Cheremissian
Votiak
Mordvinian
Magyar
2. Turkish-Tataric
Turkish (Osmanli)
Kirghizic
Bashkirian
Tataric
Kumykian
Chuvashian
Karachaic
Nogaic
Karapapakian
Kizilbashian
Tahtajic
3. Mongolian
Kalmuckian

III. SEMITIC
Arabic
Maltese
Syrian

IV. HAMITIC
Berber

V. CAUCASIC
Caucasian
Northwest
Northeast
Southwest

VI. BASQUE
Basque

Copyright by Rand McNally & Company. Made in U.S.A.

A-450076-29-1-2-1-1st

30

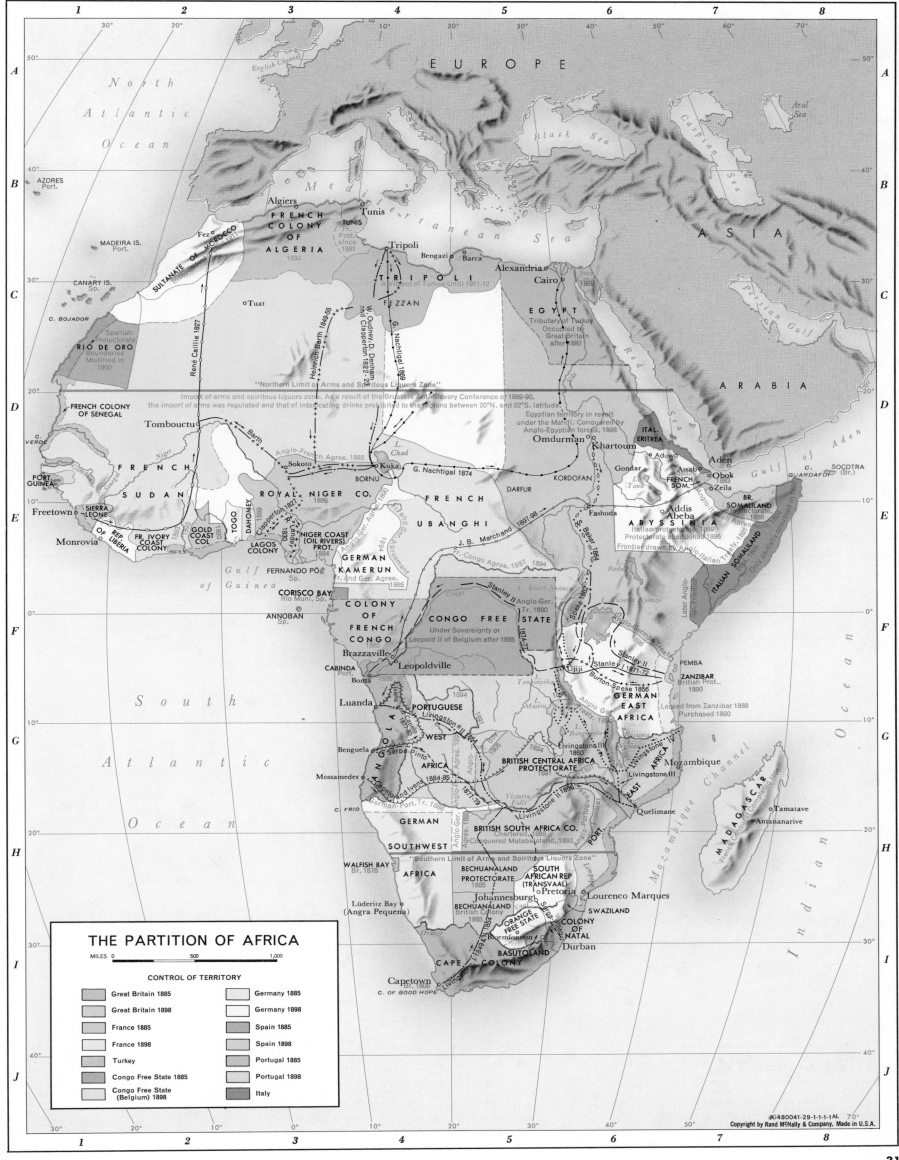

THE PARTITION OF AFRICA

MILES 0   500   1,000

CONTROL OF TERRITORY

Great Britain 1885	Germany 1885
Great Britain 1898	Germany 1898
France 1885	Spain 1885
France 1898	Spain 1898
Turkey	Portugal 1885
Congo Free State 1885	Portugal 1898
Congo Free State (Belgium) 1898	Italy

EUROPE

ASIA

North Atlantic Ocean

Mediterranean Sea

Black Sea

Caspian Sea

Aral Sea

AZORES Port.

MADEIRA IS. Port.

CANARY IS. Sp.

C. BOJADOR

C. VERDE

SULTANATE OF MOROCCO

Fez

Algiers   Tunis

TUNIS Fr. Prot. since 1881

FRENCH COLONY OF ALGERIA 1830

Tripoli

Bengazi   Barca

Alexandria

Cairo

SUEZ 1869

TRIPOLI A Vileyet of Turkey Until 1911-12

FEZZAN

EGYPT Tributary of Turkey Occupied by Great Britain after 1882

Tuat

RIO DE ORO Spanish Protectorate Boundaries Modified in 1900

FRENCH COLONY OF SENEGAL

René Caillié 1827

Tombouctu

"Northern Limit of Arms and Spiritous Liquors Zone"

Import of arms and spiritous liquors zone. As a result of the Brussels Anti-Slavery Conference of 1889-90, the import of arms was regulated and that of intoxicating drinks prohibited to the regions between 20°N. and 22°S. latitude.

Egyptian territory in revolt under the Mahdi. Conquered by Anglo-Egyptian forces, 1898

Omdurman

Khartoum

ITAL. ERITREA

ARABIA

Red Sea

Gulf of Aden

Aden

C. GUARDAFUI

SOCOTRA (Br.)

Anglo-French Agree. 1893

FRENCH SUDAN

Sokoto

BORNU

Kuka

ROYAL NIGER CO. 1886

G. Nachtigal 1874

FRENCH UBANGHI

DARFUR

KORDOFAN

Gondar

L. Tana

FRENCH SOM. 1888

Assab 1883

Obok

Zeila

BR. SOMALILAND 1884

Addis Abeba

Fashoda

ABYSSINIA Italian protectorate 1889 Protectorate abandoned 1896 Frontier drawn by Anglo-Italian

ITALIAN SOMALILAND

PORT. GUINEA

SIERRA LEONE

Freetown

REP. OF LIBERIA

Monrovia

FR. IVORY COAST

GOLD COAST COL.

TOGO

DAHOMEY

Clapperton 1827

LAGOS COLONY

NIGER COAST (OIL RIVERS) PROT. 1884

GERMAN KAMERUN

FERNANDO PO Sp.

CORISCO BAY Rio Muni, Sp.

ANNOBAN Sp.

Gulf of Guinea

COLONY OF FRENCH CONGO 1885

Brazzaville

CABINDA Port.

Boma

Leopoldville

CONGO FREE STATE 1874-77 Under Sovereignty of Leopold II of Belgium after 1885

Stanley II Anglo-Ger. Tr. 1890

L. Albert Nyanza

Speke 1860

L. Victoria Nyanza

Stanley II

Stanley I 1871-72

Burton-Speke 1856

Ujiji

PEMBA

ZANZIBAR British Prot. 1890

Leased from Zanzibar 1888 Purchased 1890

South Atlantic Ocean

Luanda

Benguela

Mossamedes

C. FRIO

PORTUGUESE WEST AFRICA

ANGOLA 1885

Serpa Pinto

L. Tanganyika

L. Mweru

L. Bangueolo

GERMAN EAST AFRICA

BRITISH CENTRAL AFRICA PROTECTORATE 1891

Livingstone III 1860

L. Nyassa

Mozambique

PORTUGUESE EAST AFRICA

Livingstone III

Quelimane

Victoria Falls

BRITISH SOUTH AFRICA CO. Chartered 1889 Conquered Matabeleland, 1893

German-Port. Tr. 1886

GERMAN SOUTHWEST AFRICA

"Southern Limit of Arms and Spiritous Liquors Zone"

WALFISH BAY Br. 1878

Lüderitz Bay (Angra Pequena)

BECHUANALAND PROTECTORATE 1885

BECHUANALAND British Colony 1885

Johannesburg

SOUTH AFRICAN REP (TRANSVAAL)

Pretoria

Lourenco Marques

SWAZILAND

ORANGE FREE STATE

Bloemfontein

BASUTOLAND

Durban

COLONY OF NATAL

CAPE COLONY

Capetown Br. 1806

C. OF GOOD HOPE

MADAGASCAR French Colony Completed 1896

Tamatave

Antananarive

Mozambique Channel

Indian Ocean

A 480041-29-1-1-1-1 AL

Copyright by Rand McNally & Company, Made in U.S.A.

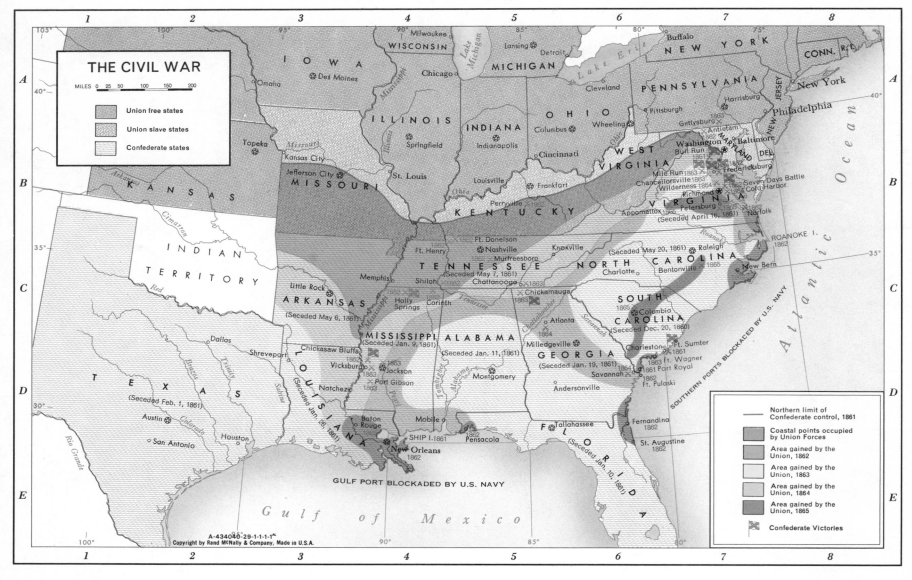

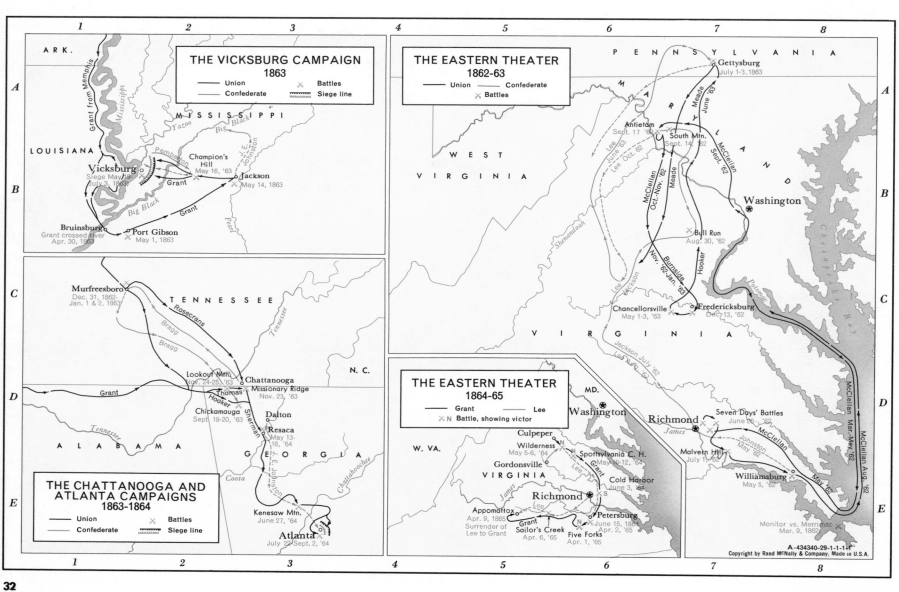

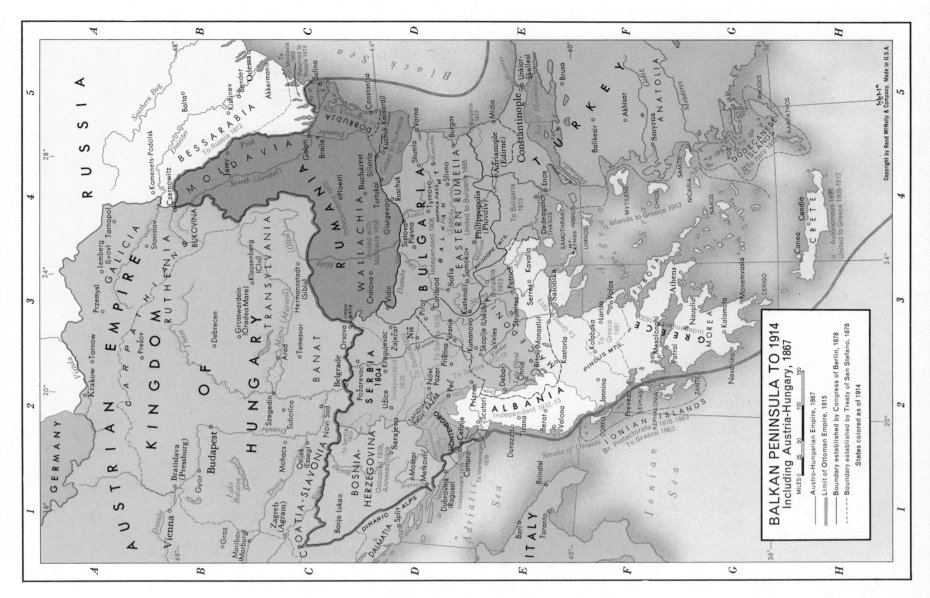

BALKAN PENINSULA TO 1914
Including Austria-Hungary, 1867

MILES 0   25   50   100   150

▬▬▬ Austro-Hungarian Empire, 1867
▬▬▬ Limit of Ottoman Empire, 1815
▬▬▬ Boundary established by Congress of Berlin, 1878
- - - Boundary established by Treaty of San Stefano, 1878
States colored as of 1914

Copyright by Rand McNally & Company, Made in U.S.A.

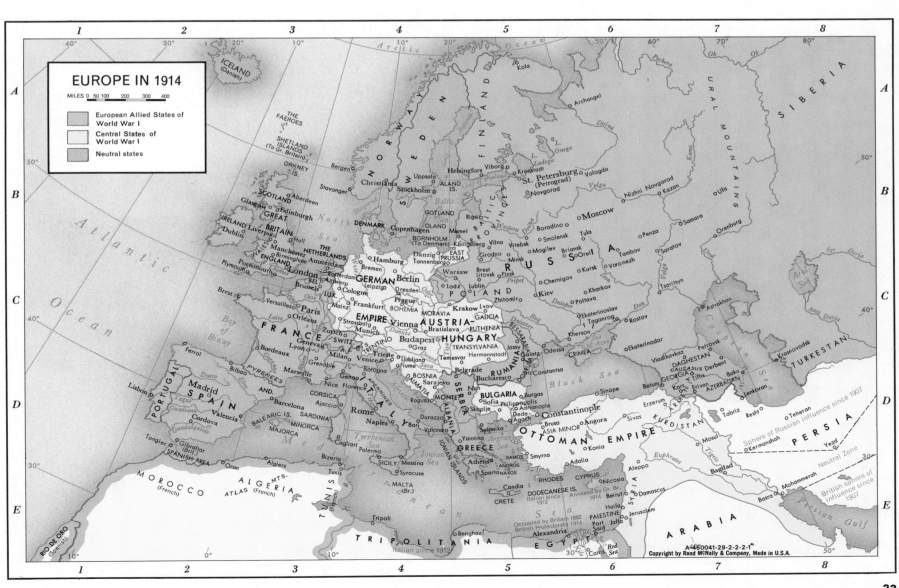

EUROPE IN 1914

MILES 0 50 100   200   300   400

A 4450041-29-2-2-2-1"
Copyright by Rand McNally & Company, Made in U.S.A.

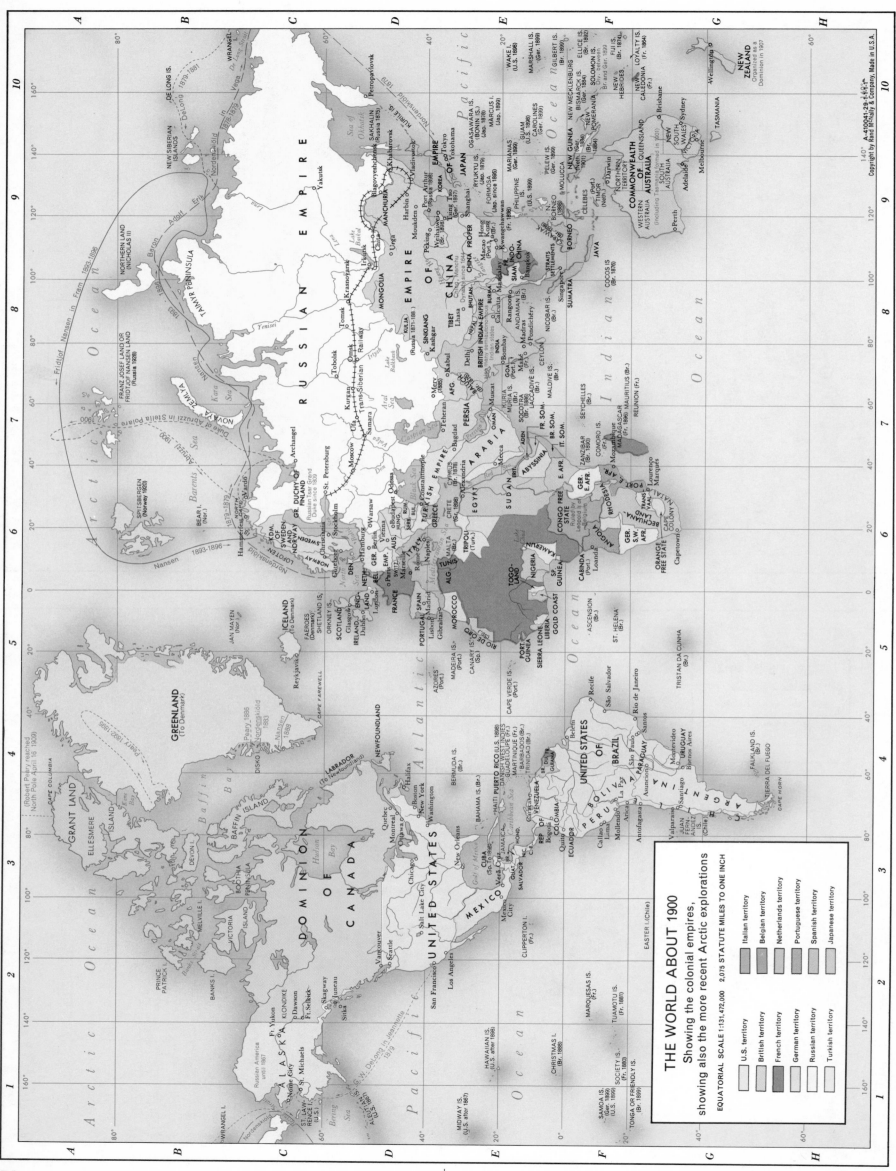

THE WORLD ABOUT 1900
Showing the colonial empires,
showing also the more recent Arctic explorations

EQUATORIAL SCALE 1:131,472,000   2,075 STATUTE MILES TO ONE INCH

U.S. territory	Italian territory
British territory	Belgian territory
French territory	Netherlands territory
German territory	Portuguese territory
Russian territory	Spanish territory
Turkish territory	Japanese territory

A-41004-1-29-1-1/2-4
Copyright by Rand McNally & Company, Made in U.S.A.

34

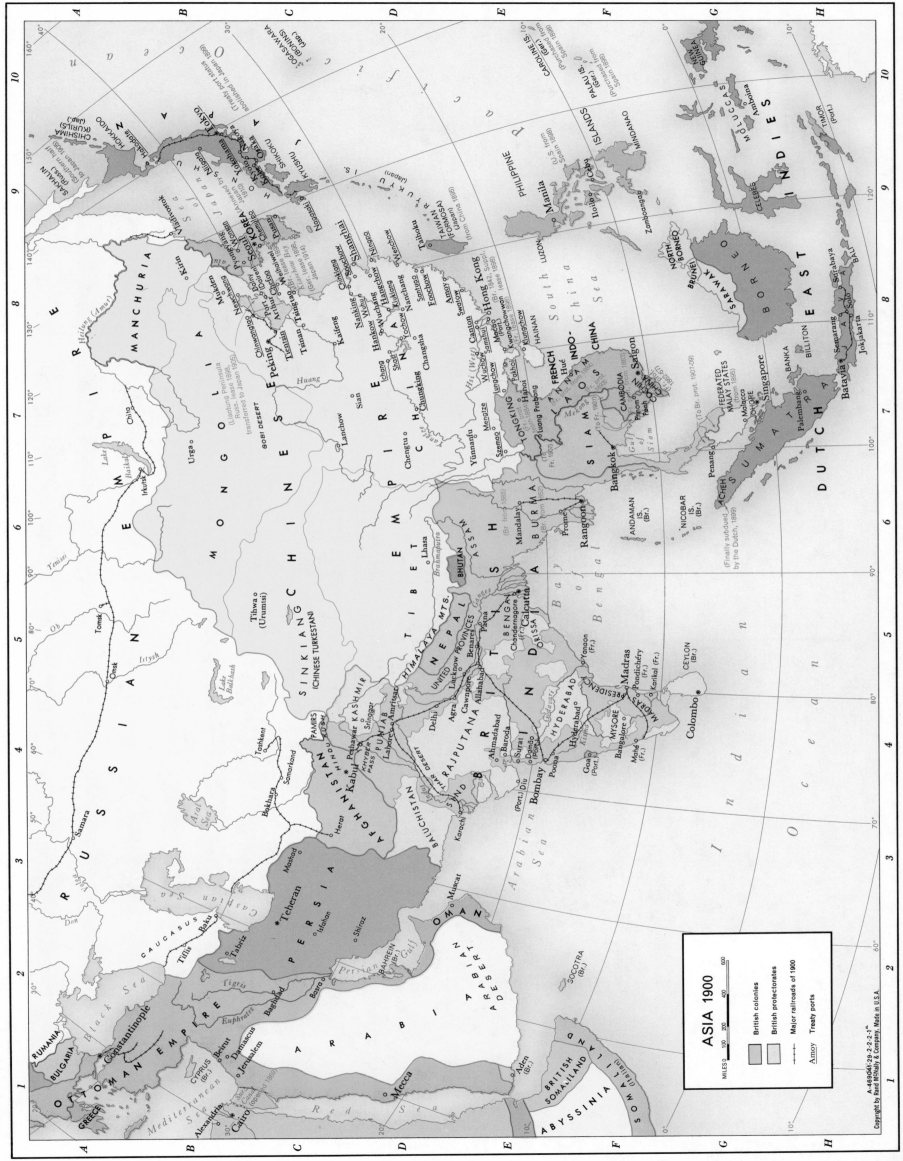

ASIA 1900

MILES 0 100 200 400 600

■ British colonies
□ British protectorates
—|— Major railroads of 1900
Amoy Treaty ports

A-469:G41-29-2-2-2-1¹

Copyright by Rand McNally & Company, Made in U.S.A.

35

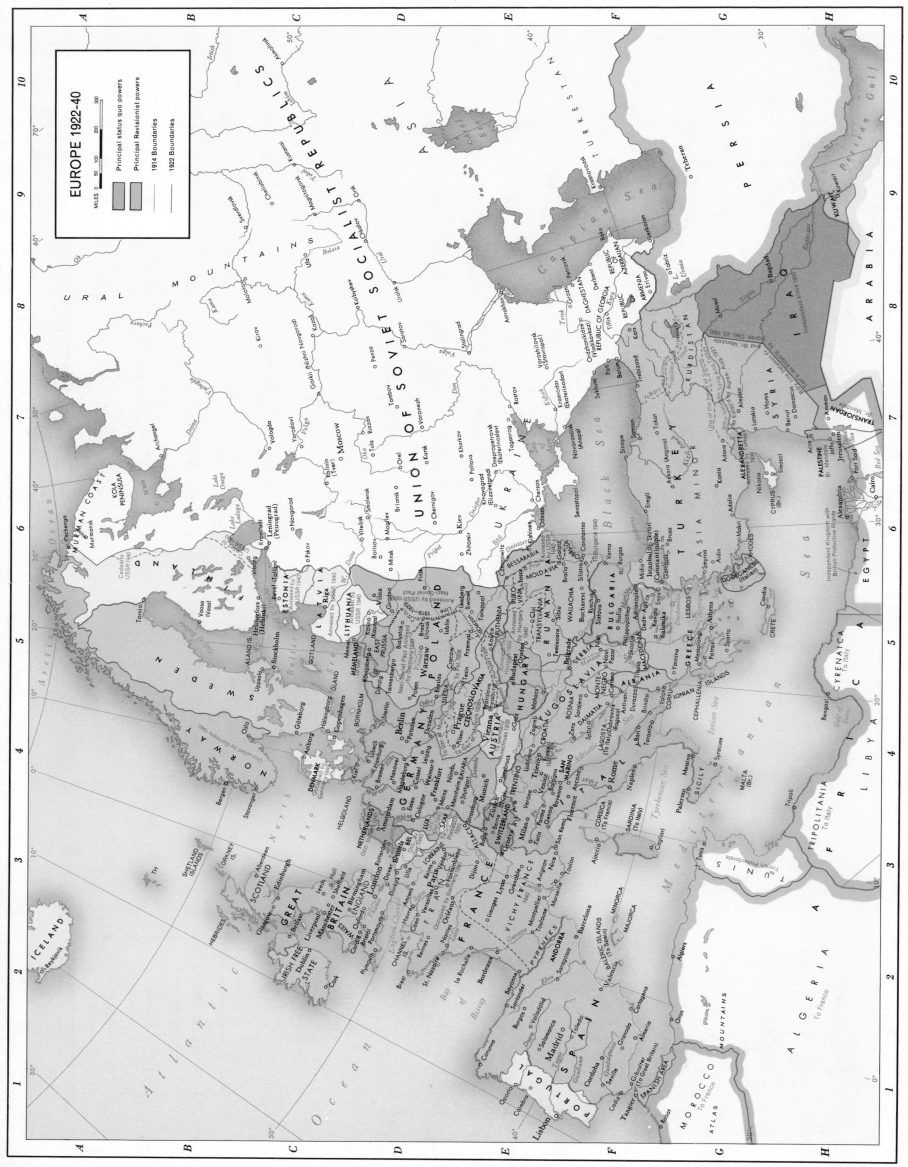

EUROPE 1922-40

Principal status quo powers
Principal Revisionist powers
1914 Boundaries
1922 Boundaries

MILES 0 50 100 200 300

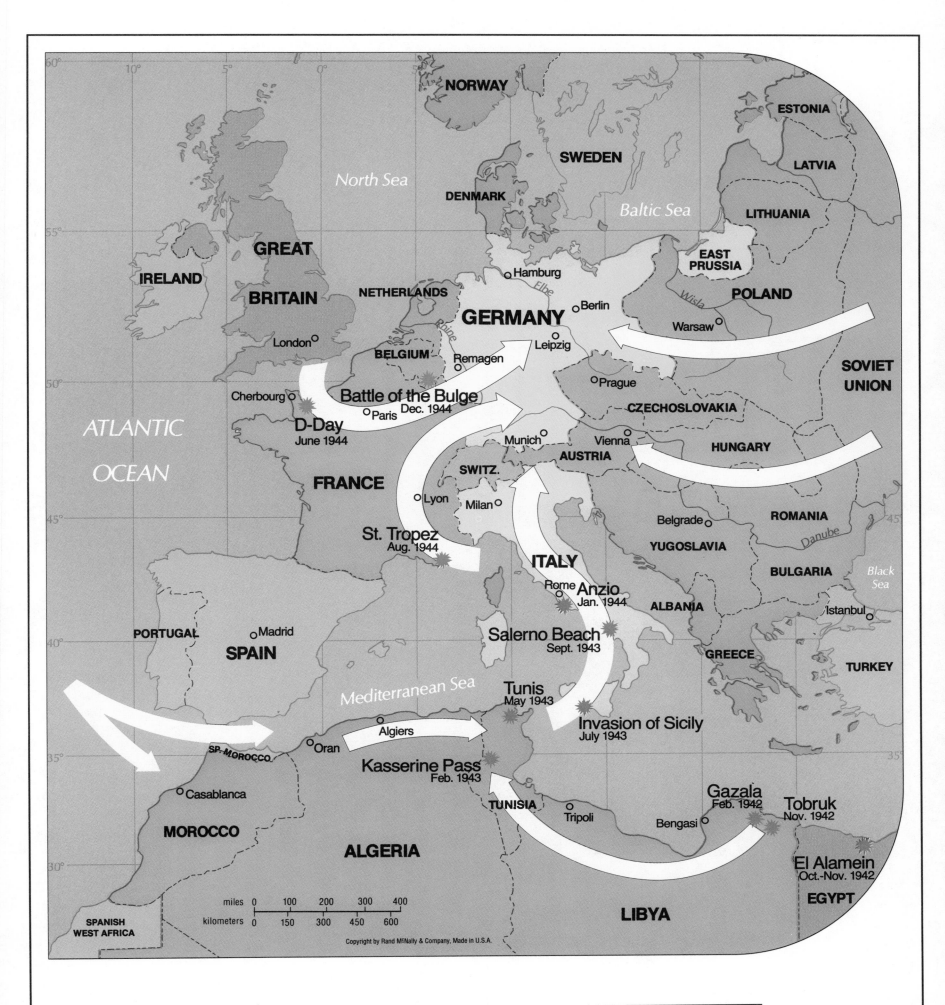

THE SECOND WORLD WAR
1941–1945

- Allied powers
- Axis powers
- Axis controlled areas
- Neutral nations
- Battles
- Allied advances

SECOND WORLD WAR CASUALTIES

Country	Battle Deaths	Wounded
Austria	280,000	350,117
Canada	32,714	53,145
France	201,568	400,000
Germany	3,250,000	7,250,000
Hungary	147,435	89,313
Italy	149,496	66,716
U.S.S.R.	6,115,000	14,012,000

Source: Information Please Almanac (Boston: Houghton Mifflin Co., 1988)

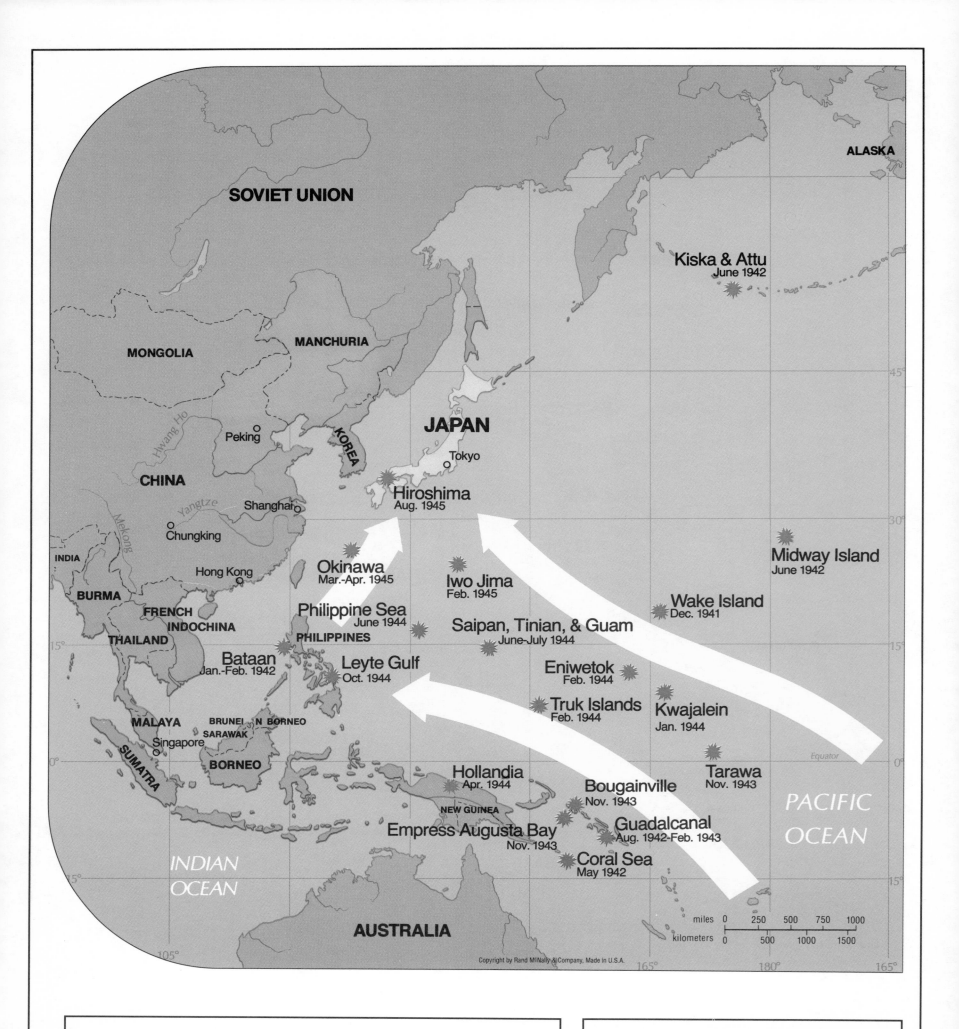

The following labels appear on the map:

ALASKA

SOVIET UNION

Kiska & Attu
June 1942

MONGOLIA

MANCHURIA

JAPAN

Peking

Tokyo

KOREA

CHINA

Hiroshima
Aug. 1945

Shanghai

Hwang Ho

Yangtze

Chungking

Midway Island
June 1942

INDIA

Hong Kong

Okinawa
Mar.-Apr. 1945

Iwo Jima
Feb. 1945

Wake Island
Dec. 1941

BURMA

Mekong

FRENCH
INDOCHINA

Philippine Sea
June 1944

Saipan, Tinian, & Guam
June-July 1944

THAILAND

PHILIPPINES

Bataan
Jan.-Feb. 1942

Leyte Gulf
Oct. 1944

Eniwetok
Feb. 1944

MALAYA

BRUNEI N BORNEO
SARAWAK

Truk Islands
Feb. 1944

Kwajalein
Jan. 1944

Singapore

SUMATRA

BORNEO

Hollandia
Apr. 1944

Tarawa
Nov. 1943

NEW GUINEA

Bougainville
Nov. 1943

Empress Augusta Bay
Nov. 1943

Guadalcanal
Aug. 1942-Feb. 1943

PACIFIC
OCEAN

Coral Sea
May 1942

INDIAN
OCEAN

Equator

AUSTRALIA

Copyright by Rand McNally & Company, Made in U.S.A.

miles 0 250 500 750 1000
kilometers 0 500 1000 1500

U. S. CASUALTIES IN SECOND WORLD WAR
1941–1946

Branch	Numbers engaged	Battle deaths	Other deaths	Total deaths	Wounds not mortal	Total casualties
Army*	11,260,000	234,874	83,400	318,274	565,861	884,135
Navy	4,183,466	36,950	25,664	62,614	37,778	100,392
Marines	669,100	19,773	4,778	24,511	67,207	91,718
Total	16,112,566	291,557	113,842	405,399	670,846	1,076,245

*Includes Air Force

Source: Information Please Almanac (Boston: Houghton Mifflin Co., 1988)

SECOND WORLD WAR CASUALTIES

Country	Battle Deaths	Wounded
Australia	26,976	180,684
China	1,324,516	1,762,006
India	32,121	64,354
Japan	1,270,000	140,000
New Zealand	11,625	17,000
United Kingdom	357,116	369,267
United States	291,557	670,846

Source: Information Please Almanac (Boston: Houghton Mifflin Co., 1988)

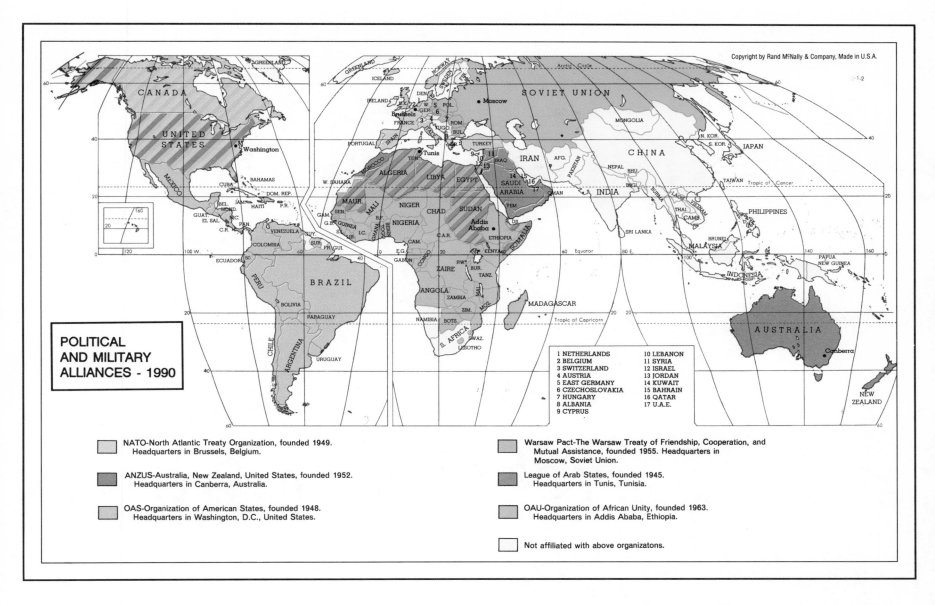

POLITICAL AND MILITARY ALLIANCES - 1990

1 NETHERLANDS	10 LEBANON
2 BELGIUM	11 SYRIA
3 SWITZERLAND	12 ISRAEL
4 AUSTRIA	13 JORDAN
5 EAST GERMANY	14 KUWAIT
6 CZECHOSLOVAKIA	15 BAHRAIN
7 HUNGARY	16 QATAR
8 ALBANIA	17 U.A.E.
9 CYPRUS	

NATO-North Atlantic Treaty Organization, founded 1949. Headquarters in Brussels, Belgium.

ANZUS-Australia, New Zealand, United States, founded 1952. Headquarters in Canberra, Australia.

OAS-Organization of American States, founded 1948. Headquarters in Washington, D.C., United States.

Warsaw Pact-The Warsaw Treaty of Friendship, Cooperation, and Mutual Assistance, founded 1955. Headquarters in Moscow, Soviet Union.

League of Arab States, founded 1945. Headquarters in Tunis, Tunisia.

OAU-Organization of African Unity, founded 1963. Headquarters in Addis Ababa, Ethiopia.

Not affiliated with above organizatons.

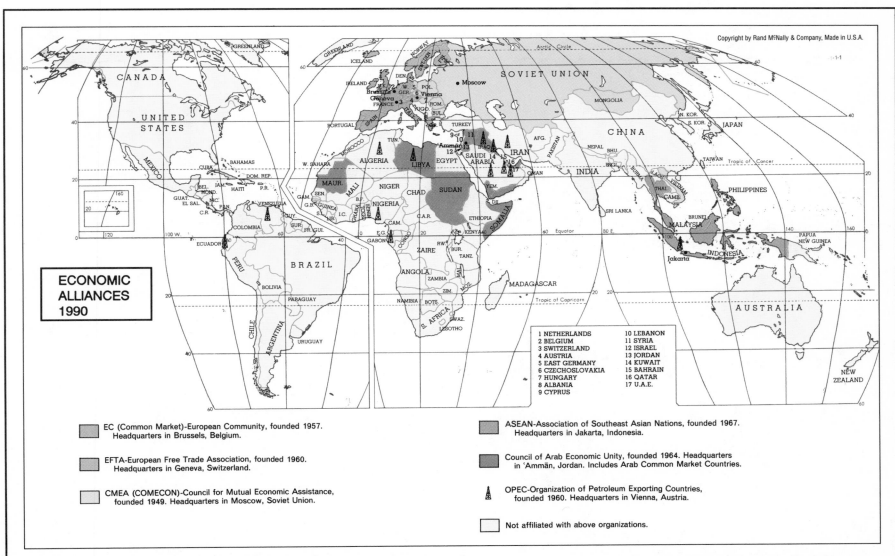

ECONOMIC ALLIANCES 1990

1 NETHERLANDS	10 LEBANON
2 BELGIUM	11 SYRIA
3 SWITZERLAND	12 ISRAEL
4 AUSTRIA	13 JORDAN
5 EAST GERMANY	14 KUWAIT
6 CZECHOSLOVAKIA	15 BAHRAIN
7 HUNGARY	16 QATAR
8 ALBANIA	17 U.A.E.
9 CYPRUS	

EC (Common Market)-European Community, founded 1957. Headquarters in Brussels, Belgium.

EFTA-European Free Trade Association, founded 1960. Headquarters in Geneva, Switzerland.

CMEA (COMECON)-Council for Mutual Economic Assistance, founded 1949. Headquarters in Moscow, Soviet Union.

ASEAN-Association of Southeast Asian Nations, founded 1967. Headquarters in Jakarta, Indonesia.

Council of Arab Economic Unity, founded 1964. Headquarters in 'Ammān, Jordan. Includes Arab Common Market Countries.

OPEC-Organization of Petroleum Exporting Countries, founded 1960. Headquarters in Vienna, Austria.

Not affiliated with above organizations.

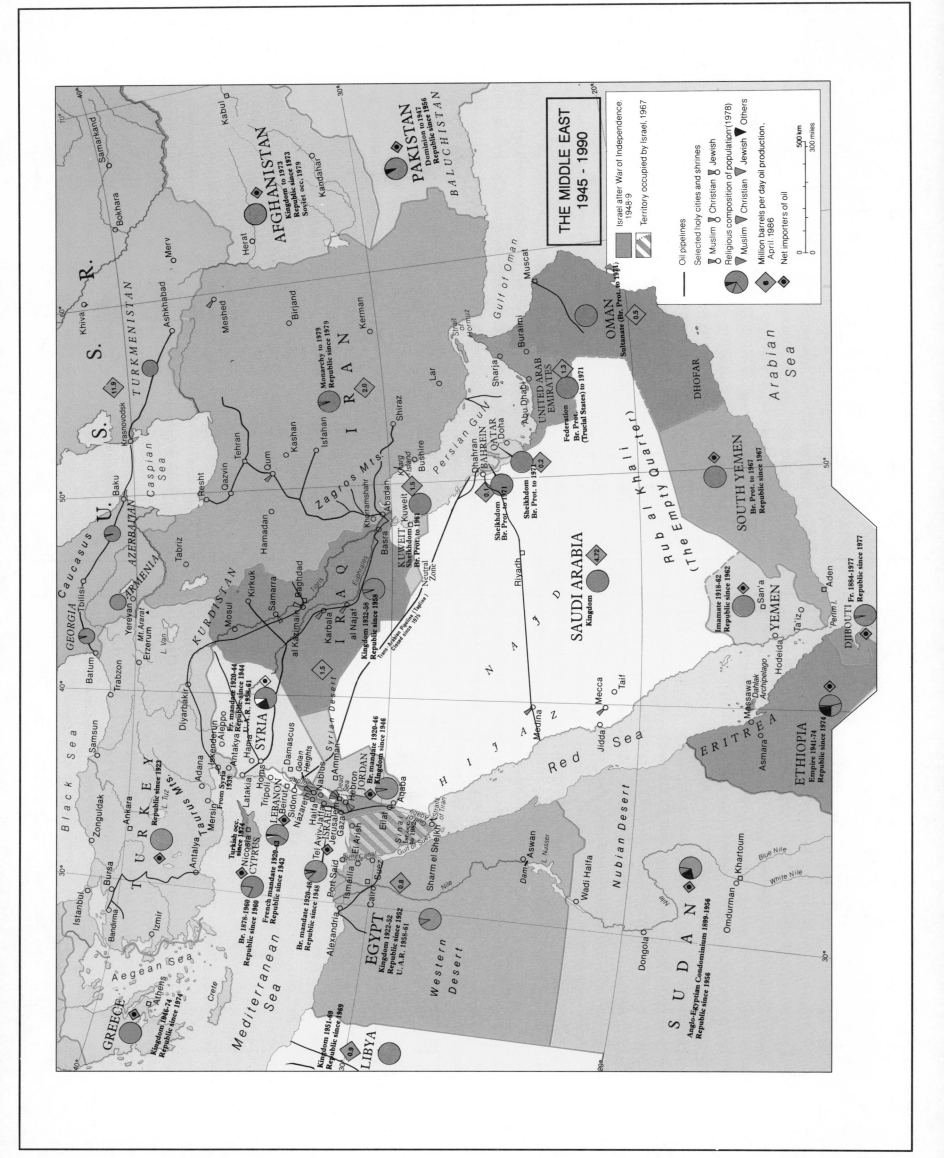

THE MIDDLE EAST
1945 - 1990

Israel after War of Independence,
1948-9

Territory occupied by Israel, 1967

Oil pipelines

Selected holy cities and shrines

Muslim   Christian   Jewish

Religious composition of population (1978)

Muslim   Christian   Jewish   Others

Million barrels per day oil production,
April 1986

Net importers of oil

500 km
300 miles

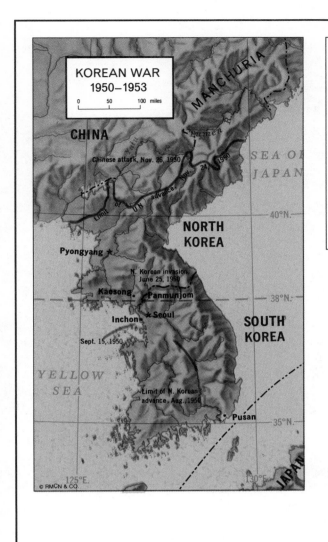

KOREAN WAR
1950–1953

0   50   100 miles

CHINA

MANCHURIA

Chinese attack, Nov. 26, 1950

SEA OF JAPAN

40°N.

NORTH KOREA

Pyongyang ★

N. Korean invasion June 25, 1950

Kaesong ★
Panmunjom ★
Sept. 15, 1950

Inchon ★
★ Seoul

SOUTH KOREA

38°N.

YELLOW SEA

Limit of N. Korean advance, Aug. 1950

35°N.

★ Pusan

JAPAN

125°E.   130°E.

© RMCN & CO.

VIETNAM WAR CASUALTIES

United States

Battle deaths	47,382
Wounded	153,303
Died, non-combat	1,811
Missing, captured	10,753

South Vietnam

Military killed in action	110,357
Military wounded	499,026
Civilian killed	415,000
Civilian wounded	913,000

Communists Regulars and Guerillas

Killed in action	666,000

Source: U.S. Department of Defense

KOREAN WAR CASUALTIES

United States

Killed	54,246
Wounded	103,284

Republic of Korea

Killed	415,004
Wounded	428,568

United Nations

Killed and wounded	15,465

China

Killed and wounded	900,000

North Korea

Killed and wounded	520,000

Source: U.S. Department of Defense

CHINA

Dien Bien Phu

NORTH VIETNAM

LAOS

HANOI ⊡

THAILAND

Hai Phong   Tonkin Gulf Incident

VIETIANE ⊡

GULF OF TONKIN

VIETNAM WAR
1957–1975

DMZ (Demilitarized Zone)

HO CHI MINH TRAIL

Khe Sanh
Hue
Da Nang

BANGKOK

Mekong River

CAMBODIA

★ Pleiku

SOUTH VIETNAM

PHNUM PENH ⊡

SAIGON ★ (Ho Chi Minh City)

Cam Ranh Bay

GULF OF THAILAND

Mekong Delta

SOUTH CHINA SEA

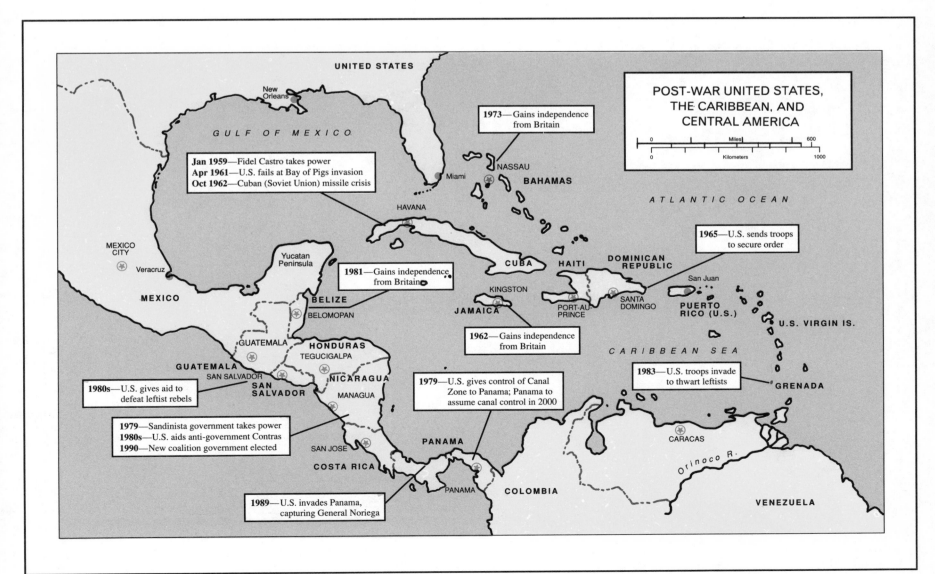

UNITED STATES

New Orleans

GULF OF MEXICO

1973—Gains independence from Britain

POST-WAR UNITED STATES, THE CARIBBEAN, AND CENTRAL AMERICA

0   Miles   600
0   Kilometers   1000

Jan 1959—Fidel Castro takes power
Apr 1961—U.S. fails at Bay of Pigs invasion
Oct 1962—Cuban (Soviet Union) missile crisis

NASSAU

Miami   BAHAMAS

ATLANTIC OCEAN

HAVANA

MEXICO CITY

Veracruz

MEXICO

Yucatan Peninsula

1981—Gains independence from Britain

BELIZE
BELOMOPAN

CUBA   HAITI   DOMINICAN REPUBLIC

San Juan

1965—U.S. sends troops to secure order

KINGSTON

JAMAICA

PORT-AU-PRINCE   SANTA DOMINGO

PUERTO RICO (U.S.)

U.S. VIRGIN IS.

1962—Gains independence from Britain

CARIBBEAN SEA

GUATEMALA

HONDURAS
TEGUCIGALPA

GUATEMALA
SAN SALVADOR

1983—U.S. troops invade to thwart leftists

GRENADA

1980s—U.S. gives aid to defeat leftist rebels

SAN SALVADOR

NICARAGUA

MANAGUA

1979—U.S. gives control of Canal Zone to Panama; Panama to assume canal control in 2000

1979—Sandinista government takes power
1980s—U.S. aids anti-government Contras
1990—New coalition government elected

SAN JOSE

COSTA RICA

PANAMA

PANAMA

CARACAS

Orinoco R.

COLOMBIA

VENEZUELA

1989—U.S. invades Panama, capturing General Noriega

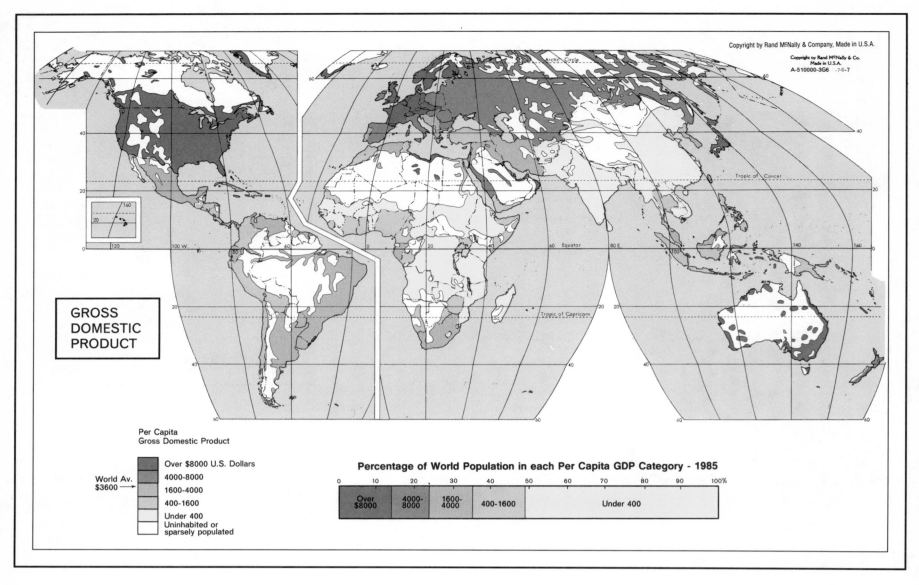

GROSS DOMESTIC PRODUCT

Per Capita
Gross Domestic Product

Over $8000 U.S. Dollars
4000-8000
World Av.
$3600 → 1600-4000
400-1600
Under 400
Uninhabited or
sparsely populated

Percentage of World Population in each Per Capita GDP Category - 1985

0	10	20	30	40	50	60	70	80	90	100%

Over $8000	4000-8000	1600-4000	400-1600	Under 400

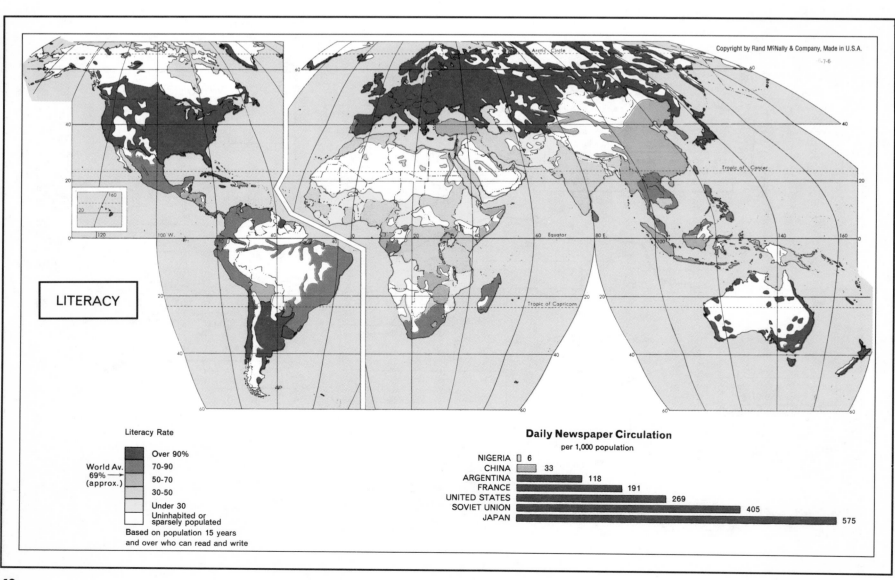

LITERACY

Literacy Rate

Over 90%
70-90
World Av.
69% → 50-70
(approx.)
30-50
Under 30
Uninhabited or
sparsely populated

Based on population 15 years
and over who can read and write

Daily Newspaper Circulation
per 1,000 population

Country	Circulation
NIGERIA	6
CHINA	33
ARGENTINA	118
FRANCE	191
UNITED STATES	269
SOVIET UNION	405
JAPAN	575

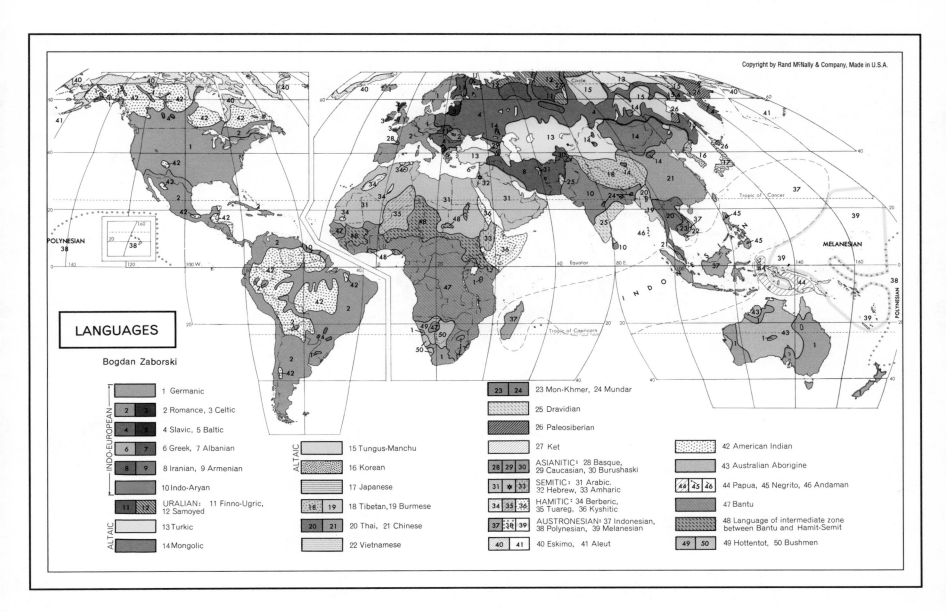

LANGUAGES

Bogdan Zaborski

INDO-EUROPEAN
- 1 Germanic
- 2 Romance, 3 Celtic
- 4 Slavic, 5 Baltic
- 6 Greek, 7 Albanian
- 8 Iranian, 9 Armenian
- 10 Indo-Aryan

URALIAN: 11 Finno-Ugric, 12 Samoyed

ALTAIC
- 13 Turkic
- 14 Mongolic
- 15 Tungus-Manchu
- 16 Korean
- 17 Japanese
- 18 Tibetan, 19 Burmese
- 20 Thai, 21 Chinese
- 22 Vietnamese

- 23 Mon-Khmer, 24 Mundar
- 25 Dravidian
- 26 Paleosiberian
- 27 Ket

ASIANITIC: 28 Basque, 29 Caucasian, 30 Burushaski

SEMITIC: 31 Arabic, 32 Hebrew, 33 Amharic

HAMITIC: 34 Berberic, 35 Tuareg, 36 Kyshitic

AUSTRONESIAN: 37 Indonesian, 38 Polynesian, 39 Melanesian

- 40 Eskimo, 41 Aleut
- 42 American Indian
- 43 Australian Aborigine
- 44 Papua, 45 Negrito, 46 Andaman
- 47 Bantu
- 48 Language of intermediate zone between Bantu and Hamit-Semit
- 49 Hottentot, 50 Bushmen

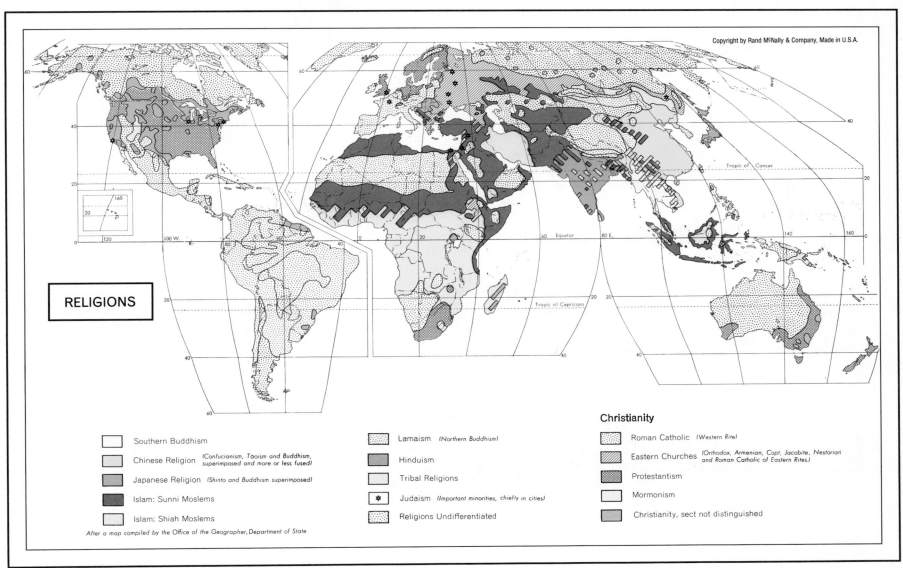

RELIGIONS

- Southern Buddhism
- Chinese Religion (Confucianism, Taoism and Buddhism, superimposed and more or less fused)
- Japanese Religion (Shinto and Buddhism superimposed)
- Islam: Sunni Moslems
- Islam: Shiah Moslems
- Lamaism (Northern Buddhism)
- Hinduism
- Tribal Religions
- Judaism (Important minorities, chiefly in cities)
- Religions Undifferentiated

Christianity
- Roman Catholic (Western Rite)
- Eastern Churches (Orthodox, Armenian, Copt, Jacobite, Nestorian and Roman Catholic of Eastern Rites.)
- Protestantism
- Mormonism
- Christianity, sect not distinguished

After a map compiled by the Office of the Geographer, Department of State

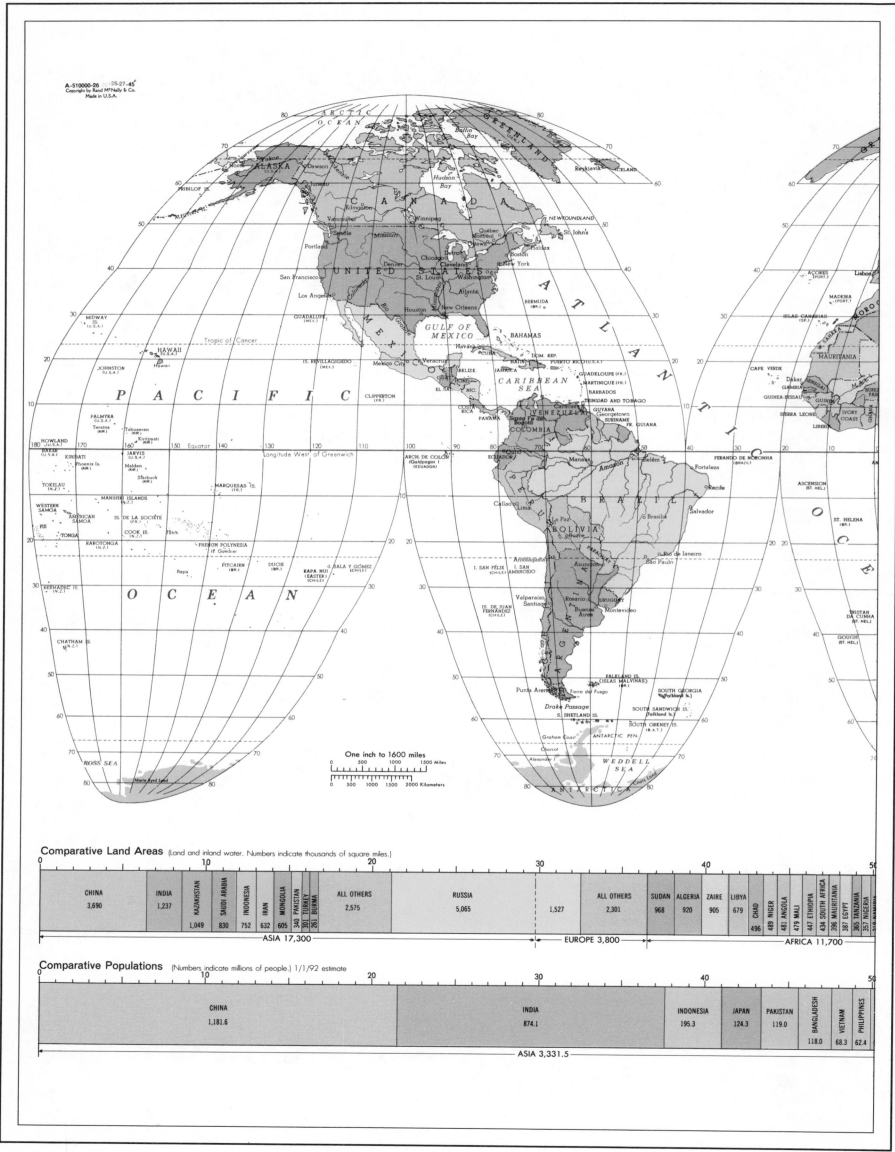

One inch to 1600 miles

0 500 1000 1500 Miles

0 500 1000 1500 2000 Kilometers

Comparative Land Areas (Land and inland water. Numbers indicate thousands of square miles.)

0	10	20	30	40	50

| CHINA 3,690 | INDIA 1,237 | KAZAKHSTAN 1,049 | SAUDI ARABIA 830 | INDONESIA 752 | IRAN 632 | MONGOLIA 605 | PAKISTAN 340 | TURKEY 301 | BURMA 261 | ALL OTHERS 2,575 | RUSSIA 5,065 | 1,527 | ALL OTHERS 2,301 | SUDAN 968 | ALGERIA 920 | ZAIRE 905 | LIBYA 679 | CHAD 496 | NIGER 489 | ANGOLA 481 | MALI 479 | ETHIOPIA 447 | SOUTH AFRICA 434 | MAURITANIA 396 | EGYPT 387 | TANZANIA 365 | NIGERIA 357 |

ASIA 17,300 ← → EUROPE 3,800 ← → AFRICA 11,700

Comparative Populations (Numbers indicate millions of people.) 1/1/92 estimate

0	10	20	30	40	50

| CHINA 1,181.6 | INDIA 874.1 | INDONESIA 195.3 | JAPAN 124.3 | PAKISTAN 119.0 | BANGLADESH 118.0 | VIETNAM 68.3 | PHILIPPINES 62.4 |

ASIA 3,331.5

44

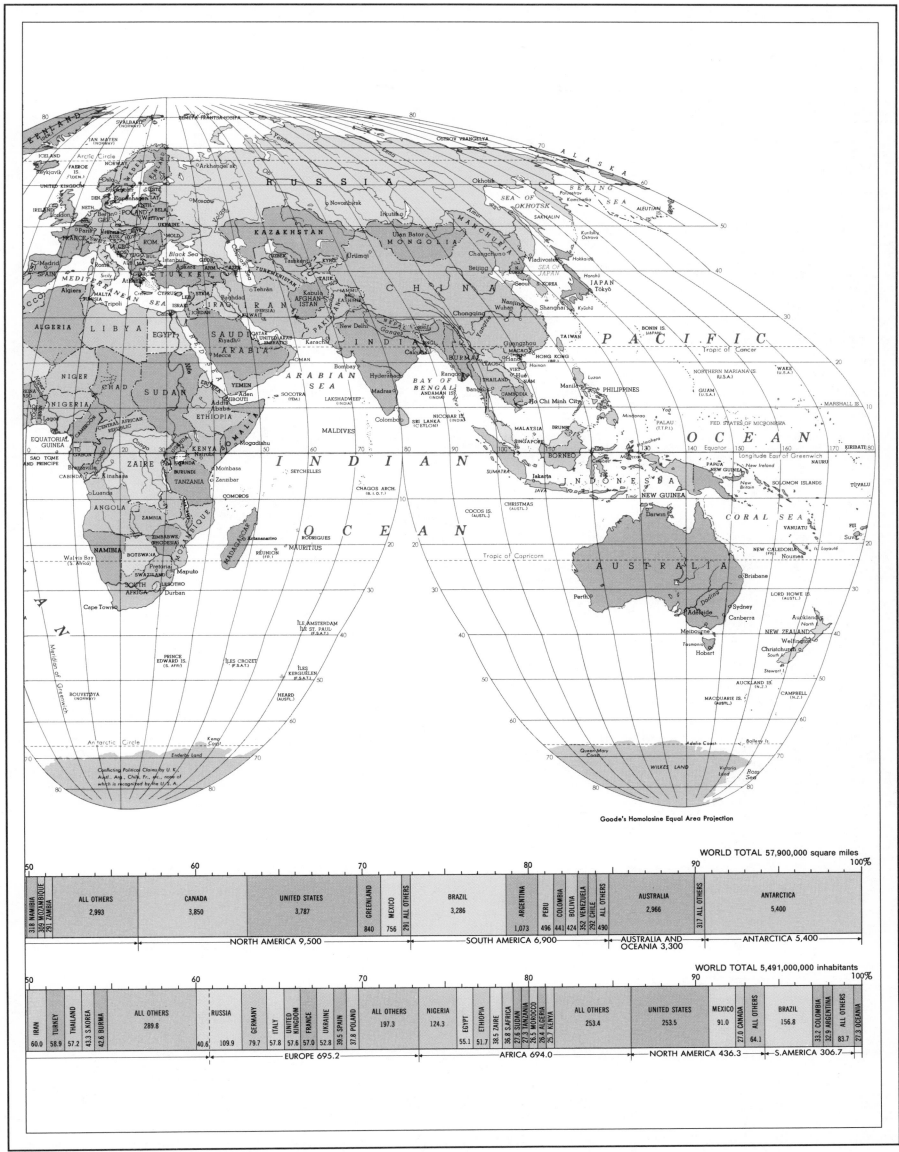

Goode's Homolosine Equal Area Projection

INDEX

The following index lists important place names appearing on the maps in the *Historical Atlas of the World*. Countries and regions are indexed to the several maps which portray their areal and political development at successive periods. In general, each index entry includes a map reference key and the page number of the map. Where two maps fall on one page, the letter "a" or "b" following the page number refers to the top or bottom map, respectively. Alternate names and spellings are added in parentheses.